Oak Island Family

Oak Island Family

The Restall Hunt for Buried Treasure

Lee Lamb

DUNDURN
TORONTO

Editor: Allison Hirst
Design: Courtney Horner
Printer: Webcom

Library and Archives Canada Cataloguing in Publication

Lamb, Lee
    Oak Island family : the Restall hunt for
buried treasure / Lee Lamb.

Issued also in electronic formats.
ISBN 978-1-4597-0342-1

    1. Oak Island Treasure Site (N.S.)--Juvenile literature.
2. Restall family--Juvenile literature. 3. Treasure troves--Nova
Scotia--Oak Island (Lunenburg)--History--Juvenile literature.
I. Title.

FC2345.O23L36 2012   j971.6'23   C2012-900143-0

1   2   3   4   5   16   15   14   13   12

 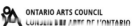

We acknowledge the support of the **Canada Council for the Arts** and the **Ontario Arts Council** for our publishing program. We also acknowledge the financial support of the **Government of Canada** through the **Canada Book Fund** and **Livres Canada Books**, and the **Government of Ontario** through the **Ontario Book Publishing Tax Credit** and the **Ontario Media Development Corporation**.

Care has been taken to trace the ownership of copyright material used in this book. The author and the publisher welcome any information enabling them to rectify any references or credits in subsequent editions.

J. Kirk Howard, President

Printed and bound in Canada.
www.dundurn.com

Dundurn
3 Church Street, Suite 500
Toronto, Ontario, Canada
M5E 1M2

Gazelle Book Services Limited
White Cross Mills
High Town, Lancaster, England
LA1 4XS

Dundurn
2250 Military Road
Tonawanda, NY
U.S.A. 14150

Contents

Acknowledgements

This book would not have been possible without the letters, journals, essays, photographs, maps, and sketches left by my family members who lived the Restall hunt for treasure. Thank you to Eddie Sparham for saving the letters my father wrote to his father, and for sharing them with me. They gave me insight into my family's experience far beyond what I could have learned without them.

Very special thanks also go to Wayne McElhone, whose advice and encouragement helped me to prepare the Restall story for a teen audience; to Ann MacIntyre, who always provided a different viewpoint, which I truly appreciate; to Marilyn McCarthy, who was kind enough to take a last look at the manuscript and offer helpful suggestions; and to my brother Rick, who was generous in offering Restall insights — I greatly value his contributions and ongoing encouragement. Last, of course, I am grateful to Beth Bruder and the hard-working staff at Dundurn for believing in this project.

Introduction

People from all over the world seem to know about Canada's Oak Island. And yet many Canadians do not. Amazing discoveries, personal sacrifice, and human tragedy are just a few of the ingredients that make the Oak Island story one that deserves to be remembered.

Oak Island lies in Mahone Bay on the Atlantic coast of Canada. Buried deep within the island is a treasure so immense that no one can even guess how much it is worth. At least, that is what some people believe. And that is why, for more than 200 years, treasure hunters have come to Oak Island and have spent fortunes attempting to tame the island and claim the treasure.

The Restall family — my father, mother, and two brothers — were among those treasure hunters. Their Oak Island adventure is told here. The events that many years ago started the hunt for treasure on the island, and the stories of searchers who went before the Restalls are included, too. This book was written especially for teenage readers and for adult, first-time readers of Oak Island lore.

This is the story of Oak Island and of the Restalls, a Canadian family who were determined to be the ones to find the treasure and solve the mystery of Oak Island. They dreamed of fame and fortune. What they got was something very, very different.

Chapter One

What Would You Say?

What would you say if you were 15 years old and your father pulled you aside and said, "Your mother and I are going to California to join the circus. Do you want to come?"

You would know that you didn't *have* to go with your parents. You could stay with your sister and keep attending school instead. Now, let's see. So the choice is circus or school; California or Hamilton, Ontario; a new once-in-a-lifetime adventure or the same old routine.

Bobby Restall closed his notebook with a snap and said, "When do we leave?"

So Bobby, his five-year-old brother, Ricky, and their mom and dad packed up their motorcycles, their silk shirts, jodhpurs, and riding boots, as well as the 16 sections that made up the Globe of Death, and they piled all of it into a five-ton truck. They attached a little box trailer to the truck; then they hooked their 20-foot house trailer to their old Packard and set off on their Great American Circus Adventure.

But *that* is a story for another time.

I mention it here only so you can understand that the Restalls were not your average family. They had big dreams and a love of adventure. But they didn't just dream, they actually did things that were quite out of the ordinary.

Now, what would you say if you were that same young man, now 18 years old? For seven months you had travelled the west coast of the United States with your parents and their Globe of Death motorcycle act as the starring attraction

The Globe of Death, circa 1957.

for Pollock Brothers Circus. You had driven one of the rigs from city to city, you had worked alongside the men assembling and disassembling the Globe, you had watched your parents and other circus artists perform, night after night, before adoring crowds. When the contract was finished, you had come back to Hamilton to return to school and help your dad. He was a certified plumber and steamfitter as well as a showman, but you helped him with his spare-time projects, such as building carnival rides. And now your father was pulling you aside again, and this time he was saying, "I'm going to Oak Island in Nova Scotia to dig for treasure. I sure could use your help. Do you want to come along?"

Again, Bobby Restall didn't blink an eye before he replied, "Count me in!"

In no time, a trailer carrying a 15-foot outboard motorboat was hitched to the old Packard, and a box trailer followed behind Bobby's '47 Dodge. Bob Restall, his wife Mildred, and their son Bobby loaded up as many tools and personal belongings as the boat, trailer, and two old cars could possibly carry.

After the camera-snapping and the excited well-wishes and goodbyes were over, Ricky, Doug, and I stood in silence and watched as the car slowly drove out of sight.

Ricky was only eight years old at the time and couldn't go to Oak Island because he needed to attend school. I am Bobby and Ricky's sister, Lee. That day I was 24 years old. By that time, my husband Doug and I had our own little family — Sandy, Barry, and Brook — so there would be no Oak Island adventure for us either.

I don't mind telling you that I was just a little envious as Mom, Dad, and Bobby drove off that day on their newest adventure.

Oak Island, Nova Scotia, is the large, peanut-shaped island on the right of the photograph. The island is approximately 1.073 kilometres long and 0.8 kilometres at its widest point. The narrowing near the middle of the island is where the swamp lies. On the far right, the hooked tip of the island is where the Money Pit and Smith's Cove are found. Details from that end of the island can be seen on Bobby's map (Figure 1). Down the left edge of the photo is the mainland, which includes the community of Western Shore. The water in the gap between the island and the point of the mainland that lies closest to the island is where the Restalls rowed over to the mainland in their skiff, when bad weather prevented use of the motorboat.

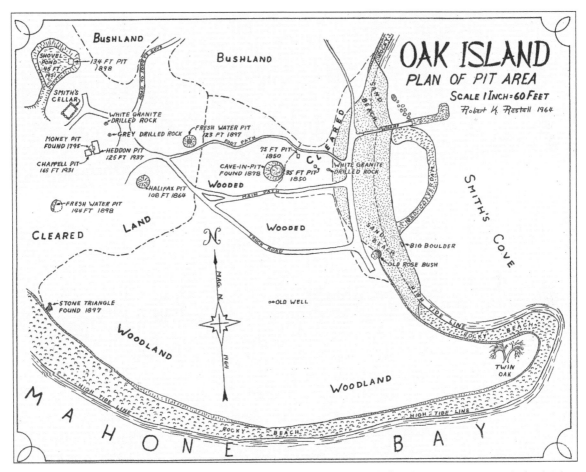

Figure 1: Bobby Restall drew this map. It shows the shafts dug by other searchers before the Restalls went to Oak Island. Take a look at the beach at Smith's Cove, the curving cofferdam in the water of the cove, and Hedden's Wharf. Inland, almost all pits and markers are located on a plateau, or "clearing" that is 32 feet above sea level. Be sure to note the round Money Pit with the rectangular Chappell Pit and Hedden Pit overlapping it. For a timeline of the treasure hunters who are responsible for this work on Oak Island, see Appendix 1.

Chapter Two

Treasure? What Treasure?

I'll bet that when Dad said "dig for treasure," Bobby imagined leaning into a spade and uncovering a huge chest brimming with gold and jewels. But the treasure of Oak Island was nothing like that. It would have taken more than a chest full of jewels to keep all those treasure hunters working on Oak Island for over 200 years.

My dad had read about the Oak Island treasure when he was a young man on a trip to England — before the Second World War. He never mentioned his interest in Oak Island to the family, but we later learned that for several years he had written to the owner of the island, Mel Chappell, telling him that he would like a chance to search for the treasure there. Mr. Chappell had written back to him, and although he hadn't said yes, he hadn't said no either. A few times Mr. Chappell seemed ready to let Dad have a try at the treasure, but then he would give someone else permission instead. My father was a patient man. He kept writing.

And finally, with Mr. Chappell's approval, Bob Restall was on his way, accompanied by his wife and son, to conquer Oak Island.

It's time to learn a little history about Oak Island.

Three Teenagers with Bright Eyes, Hopeful Hearts, and Bulging Muscles

Oak Island is now a Canadian landmark. But its importance might never have been uncovered if it had not been for three teenage boys — Daniel McInnis, John Smith, and Anthony Vaughan.

Legend has it that one day in 1795, Daniel McInnis, a 16-year-old who lived nearby, rowed over to Oak Island and went ashore. As he walked around, he deduced that some of the original growth of trees and bushes at the far end of the island must have been cut down some years earlier because this area was now filled with newer trees and plants.

Daniel noticed a big old oak tree that still stood among the new growth, and he saw that something was hanging from its sawed-off limb. It was a block and tackle. Daniel touched it and it fell to the ground in pieces, so he knew that it must be very old. Under the limb from where the block and tackle had hung, he also noticed a depression in the earth.

His heart must have skipped a beat. A block and tackle is a type of pulley used to lift very heavy objects. A depression in the earth means someone has dug up the earth underneath. Daniel came to the conclusion that something must be buried there.

At the time of Daniel's discovery, many stories were told of pirates and buried treasures in this part of Canada. Perhaps that was because, in 1700, the governor of Acadia (Nova Scotia) had offered pirates safe haven in exchange for guarding the coast. It is well-recorded that on Saturday mornings pirate ships could be seen gathering together in Mahone Bay.

Figure 2: A block and tackle hangs from a tree and over a depression in the earth.

> ### Pirates
> We don't know for sure who buried the treasure on Oak Island. Various theories are discussed in a later chapter. But most of the people who have hunted for treasure on Oak Island believed it to be pirate treasure. In this book I will usually refer to those who buried the treasure as "the pirates." When I use the term "original work," I'm referring to work on the island done by these people.

> ### How Big?
> All evidence seems to point to the fact that those who buried the treasure on Oak Island used the Imperial system of measurement (feet, inches, miles). For this reason, accurate measurements are provided throughout the book in Imperial units. In some cases, approximate metric conversions are also given.

So, when Daniel McInnis saw that block and tackle and the depression in the earth, he could be forgiven if his first thought was that a pirate's treasure was buried there.

He lost no time in bringing over his good friends, John Smith, who was 19 years old, and Anthony Vaughan, who was 13, to help him dig. The three youths set to work digging up the earth under the spot where the block and tackle had hung. The entire island contained very hard clay, but the earth here was loose. That led them to believe that the ground in this location had been dug before. The boys were digging in a circular area that was about 13 feet across (nearly four metres). When they got two feet down (0.6 metres), they came to a layer of flat stones. Eagerly, they pulled out the stones, expecting to find a treasure, but what they found was only more loose earth.

So they started digging again. Ten feet (3.05 metres) beneath the stones they came to a layer of large oak logs fitted tightly together and firmly secured into the walls of the hole. The logs formed a solid platform. Surely the logs had been placed there to guard a treasure that must lie just beneath!

Although it was very hard work to dislodge the logs, the young men managed to pull them out. But what they found was not treasure. Under the platform of oak logs there was just more loose earth.

In great secrecy, all summer long, the three young men rowed out to the island and continued to dig. They dug through ten more feet of loosely packed earth and came to a second layer of oak logs. When they were able to get those out, they found another ten feet of earth and then another layer of logs.

This convinced them that they were clearing out a hole that had been dug in another time by persons unknown. The boys also had no doubt that a fabulous treasure waited for them at the bottom of that hole. But removing the earth and logs became harder and harder as they dug ever deeper. Finally, at 32 feet (9.75 metres), McInnis, Smith, and Vaughan stopped digging. They were forced to admit that this job was too difficult for them to continue on alone.

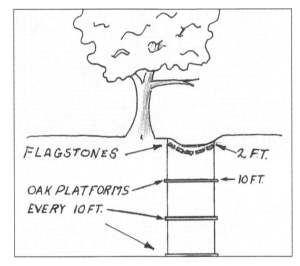

Figure 3: The Money Pit, as it was uncovered by the three teenagers.

They took several small sticks and drove them into the earth in a special formation to mark where their work had stopped. They shovelled all the earth and logs that they had worked so hard to remove back into the hole. Then, carefully, they covered all signs of their work and left the island. In time, that first shaft* would become known as the Money Pit.

Daniel McInnis, John Smith, and Anthony Vaughan would go down in history for discovering the mysterious Money Pit on Oak Island.

With their dreams of riches and their youthful energy, they had set into motion events that would make Oak Island famous well into the future and would stir the blood of would-be treasure hunters around the world.

---

* In this book, the word shaft refers to any hole that is deeper than it is wide.

Chapter Three

But There's More to the Story

Of course Bobby enjoyed hearing how the Money Pit was first discovered by the three teens. It's a story anyone would love — dreams of fabulous riches, teenage energy and hard work, and important secrets that must be kept from the adults. But before the Restalls' work could begin on the island, Bobby needed to know more about what had been discovered on Oak Island long before. The history lesson continued.

It turned out that the three discoverers of the Money Pit did not really give up on the treasure. In time, two of them bought property on the island. John Smith's house overlooked the Money Pit and Daniel McInnis purchased a lot some distance away.

After that last day of digging on the island, the boys realized they had a secret too big to keep. Eventually, they shared it with adult family members, who, in turn, quietly looked for people who would invest money to have the Money Pit dug out.

It took about seven years, but finally enough investors were found. The Onslow Company was formed, and the hunt for the treasure was on!

The Onslow Company Goes After the Treasure

In 1804, wealthy local men who were related to Anthony Vaughan formed the Onslow Company. They were just as sure as the three boys had been that pirate's treasure lay at the bottom of the Money Pit. The purpose of their newly-formed company was to get that treasure.

Daniel McInnis, John Smith, and Anthony Vaughan, by that time in their twenties, all worked on the dig.

The first task for the company was to carefully clear out the Money Pit. In doing that, they found the secret formation of sticks placed by the teens at the bottom of the hole years earlier, proving that the pit had not been disturbed since they had covered it over in 1795.

As the Onslow crew dug down into the pit, they, too, came to a layer of previously-dug earth followed by a platform of oak logs, again and again, every ten feet. But three more substances were also found. Those were coconut fibre, charcoal, and putty. The putty was smeared on some of the oak log platforms. The coconut fibre formed separate layers next to some of the platforms.

Coconuts do not grow in Canada, but coconut fibre, the hairs from around a coconut shell, was known to be used by some ships as a packing material to keep cargo items from breaking. Finding coconut fibre in the shaft was evidence that whoever had dug the shaft and put in the log platforms had probably come from another land.

As the Onslow crew dug down, they could see pickaxe marks in the hard clay sides of the Money Pit; so while the pit was originally being dug in that solid clay, it would have been necessary to sharpen tools frequently. Charcoal could have been used by the workmen to make a small fire to keep warm or to sharpen their tools.

Putty is used as a seal to keep water out. For instance, it can be used to make glass fit tightly in a window frame.

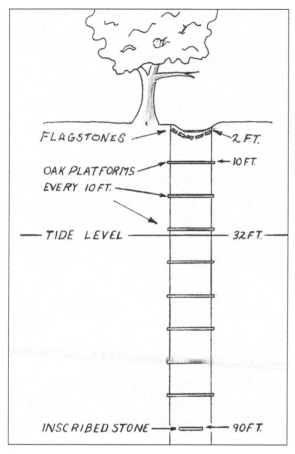

FLAGSTONES ——→   ←2 FT.

OAK PLATFORMS——   ← 10 FT.
EVERY 10 FT. ——→

—— TIDE LEVEL ——   —— 32 FT. ——

INSCRIBED STONE ——→   ←— 90 FT.

Figure 4: What the Money Pit would have looked like before the Onslow Company removed each layer.

After the Onslow crew had removed many layers of material from the Money Pit, they came to a large, heavy stone of a type not found on the island. The stone bore symbols and numbers. The markings on the stone have never officially been translated into English, although one university professor declared that the inscription read, "Ten feet below 2,000,000 pounds lie buried." (That would be British money — British Pounds Sterling.) Most people do not believe this translation is correct.

The Onslow men set the stone aside and continued to dig. At a depth of 93 feet (28.3 metres), for the first time the earth they encountered was damp. As they dug farther, so much water entered the shaft that they were forced to bail out one tub of water for every two tubs of earth.

It was late in the day when they had cleared the shaft to a depth just short of 98 feet, but before they quit work, the searchers took a crowbar and probed down into the wet earth. They struck a hard object that spanned the width of the pit. *Was it a treasure chest?* Hope was high.

When the men awoke the next morning, they found that 60 feet (18.3 metres) of water had filled the Money Pit. They immediately set to work bailing out the water, but no matter how many buckets they drew out, the water level didn't change. Eventually a pump was brought in, but in no time it burst. So, with winter setting in, it was decided that treasure hunting on Oak

Island would have to wait until the spring.

≈

In the spring of 1805, as soon as the weather allowed, the Onslow Company began work again. This time they tried a different approach. They dug a new shaft in the hard clay not far from the Money Pit — we'll call this Shaft #2.

Digging in dry earth in this new shaft, the Onslow crew dug down deeper than they had in the Money Pit. They believed the chest or vault they had struck with the crowbar the year before held the treasure they were seeking. This new shaft would allow them to tunnel horizontally from the bottom toward the Money Pit, coming up under the fabulous treasure that they imagined lay waiting for them.

But when their tunnelling got close to the Money Pit, water broke through into the new shaft with such force that the workmen had to flee for their lives. Soon, the water filled the new shaft to the same height as in the Money Pit.

The Stone in the Money Pit

It is recorded that the stone that was found became part of the fireplace in John Smith's home. Many years later it was moved to a bookbinding shop in Halifax and was displayed in the window. This coincided with shares being offered for sale to finance a dig. The stone was described by a worker/relative in the firm as being about two feet long, 15 inches wide, and ten inches thick, and weighing about 175 pounds. After being displayed, it took its place inside the shop and was used as a "beating stone and weight." By then, no evidence remained of inscription either cut or painted on the stone. Any characters had faded. In 1919, when the business was closed (the original owner was long gone), the stone could not be found.

That must have driven the men mad, especially because the Onslow Company had a bigger problem — they had run out of money. The Onslow Company's search for treasure on Oak Island was over.

The work done by the Onslow Company uncovered the fact that the layers of earth, oak logs, putty, charcoal, and coconut fibre continued for at least 90 feet into the Money Pit. From this, we can assume that if and when a treasure had been

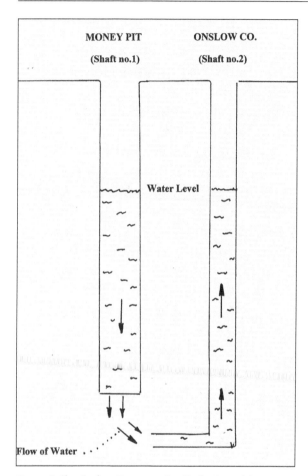

Figure 5: The Onslow Company dug Shaft #2, and then tunnelled out from the bottom of it toward the Money Pit in an attempt to come up under the treasure. Water broke through from the Money Pit and both shafts filled with water to the same level.

buried there, many workmen would have had to have been involved.

But there was a new twist to the Oak Island Mystery. Somehow, water was coming into the Money Pit with enough force to destroy the work being done. Other questions remained unanswered: Who did the work on Oak Island? How did they manage to do it without being flooded out themselves as they dug into the lower depths? Had they brought the coconut fibre with them from some other place? And what was buried there that could possibly be worth such trouble?

One part of the mystery may have been cleared up — why oak logs would have been secured to the sides of the Money Pit every ten feet. After the treasure was placed in the bottom of the shaft, the pirates must have known it might be a long time before they returned to Oak Island, and they wouldn't have wanted to leave any trace of their work. So they packed the earth they had removed back into the pit. But they knew in time, it would settle. That would leave a hole at the surface deep enough to attract attention. Placing platforms of oak logs in the shaft meant that only ten feet of earth got to settle over each platform. At the surface, this little bit of settling would hardly be noticeable. Their work could go undetected.

And this would have worked … if it hadn't been for the block and tackle.

Chapter Four

Simply Amazing

In their search for treasure, the Onslow Company had added surprising new information to what was known about Oak Island. But Bobby soon learned the best was yet to come.

The Truro Company Tries for the Treasure

It was a number of years before anyone would raise enough money to tackle Oak Island again. The Truro Company began work on the island in 1849. Among their members were a number of the old Onslow Company investors, as well as a few new ones. It had been more than 50 years since the three teenagers had first discovered the Money Pit, but two of them, John Smith and Anthony Vaughan, were on-site throughout the dig.

By the time the Truro Company began their work, the Money Pit had filled with debris, so they started by clearing it out. When the Onslow Company had left the Money Pit in 1805, it was filled with water, but when work began in 1849, the pit appeared to be dry. Because it was a Sunday, however, everyone on the crew left to go to church; when they returned, the Money Pit was again filled with water, this time to a depth of 60 feet.

The men realized that the water that filled the Money Pit reached the same height as the water in Mahone Bay. In other words, water poured into the Money Pit until it reached sea level.

Despite their best efforts to bail out the water, it remained.

The water in the Money Pit made it impossible for the crew to continue digging, so they decided to use a drill to see what they might encounter at a lower level. They ran big pumps that kept the water in the Money Pit just lower than sea level. Then they built a platform partway down the pit and used a type of auger as a drill. When an auger is used, pieces or splinters of whatever you are drilling are carried up to the surface.

The results were exciting, and the men were certain that they had found evidence of the treasure! After boring down a short distance, the auger had gone through a thick spruce platform, then it had passed through two oak boxes and three oak casks that contained loose metal. (*Could these be coins?*) Beneath all of these lay another spruce platform, even thicker than the first. As well, the auger brought up three links of a gold chain, thought to be from a pocket watch.

But there was something more.

The foreman of the work crew, James Pitblado, was seen by an investor to be looking at something that resembled a jewel on the end of his auger. He apparently washed it off and put it in his pocket. When the investor demanded to see it, Pitblado refused, saying he would bring it to the directors' meeting. They never saw him again.

The following year, the Truro Company decided to sink a new shaft (#3) and to use it to bail out the water in the Money Pit. This new shaft was dug through the hardest type of red clay to a depth of 109 feet, which is lower than the spruce platform encountered in the Money Pit that they suspected held the casks of treasure. The crew then began to dig a tunnel horizontally from the bottom of this new shaft toward the Money Pit; but once again water broke through and the workmen had to scramble to get out alive.

They were using the best equipment available at that time to bail out the shafts, but the water level did not go down. That is when they made a startling discovery … the water in the new shaft and in the Money Pit was *salt* water, and the level rose and fell with the ocean tide.

Now they realized there must be a connection between the ocean and the Money Pit. They came to the conclusion that a tunnel must have been carved through the island to cause sea water to surge in and stop anyone from reaching the treasure in the Money Pit.

The Truro crew turned their attentions to Smith's Cove.

They noticed that water was bubbling up from the beach at low tide. It did not take much digging to find that at about three feet below the beach sand there was a thick layer of coconut fibre, and under that an even thicker layer of eel grass (a type of seaweed), and under that a layer of stones that were placed tightly together. It was an elaborate construction that caused this area to act like a sponge for the sea water. Soon, this part of the beach work would be referred to as the "reservoir" because it soaked up water and held it in one place.

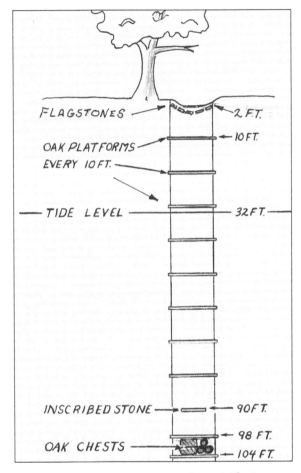

Figure 6: The Truro Company believed they had drilled through casks and boxes of treasure at the bottom of the Money Pit.

These discoveries were fascinating, but the ebb and flow of the tide made it really hard to work on the beach. It was decided that a cofferdam should be constructed to hold back the sea. A cofferdam is a water-tight structure that acts as a dam, and this one consisted of a curving wall of large stones.

Once built, the cofferdam worked perfectly, and no sea water reached Smith's Cove beach. The Truro Company was able to begin a careful examination of the beach and seabed near the shore without the tides interfering with their work. And here they made a surprising discovery. Just inside the cofferdam, after digging five feet into the seabed, they found five small drains about eight inches apart. These drains spread out from one point like a fan, or like five fingers on a hand. Each of those five "fingers" was an individual drain constructed of small, flat stones that appeared to have been shaved by a hammer so that they fit together tightly, creating passageways for sea water. The five drains converged into one larger drain that travelled inland. It was so strong and perfectly constructed that no part of it had collapsed or allowed sand to enter and obstruct it during all the years since it had been placed there.

Up on the beach, at the high-tide level, the five finger drains came together to form one larger drain, or water tunnel, just like a wrist for the five fingers.

The "Drains"

Most histories of the island refer to the five finger formations as "drains." But they do not actually drain water from the island. Instead, they are conduits, bringing sea water from Smith's Cove into the Money Pit. However, I have followed the norm and called them "drains" throughout.

The crew tried, but they could not follow that single tunnel inland toward the Money Pit because the beach was completely saturated with water. The reservoir had been constructed to draw in water and hold it for long periods of time.

Imagine how excited the Truro group must have been when they made these discoveries.

This beautifully designed beach work was the source of the water that flooded into the Money Pit. Sea water at Smith's Cove was drawn by gravity into the five finger drains, and on into the wrist-like single tunnel that passed under the beach and then travelled some 520 feet (159 metres) down through the hard clay of the island to the bottom of the Money Pit, where it flooded away every attempt to get to the treasure.

This work was an engineering marvel.

Could it have been produced by pirates? Surely the work on Oak Island would have had to be done by clever minds with high-level engineering skills. To complete this massive job, they also would have had to possess knowledge of underground tunnelling and had a small army of men at their command.

But these brilliant men from long ago had finally met their match. The Truro Company had every right to believe that with their cofferdam holding back the sea, the treasure of Oak Island would be theirs at last.

But fate had other plans.

During a raging storm one night, a very high tide swept in to Smith's Cove. The combination of high tide and storm allowed the sea to overflow the cofferdam and to surge onto the beach. The cofferdam had not been built in a way that would keep it strong if it

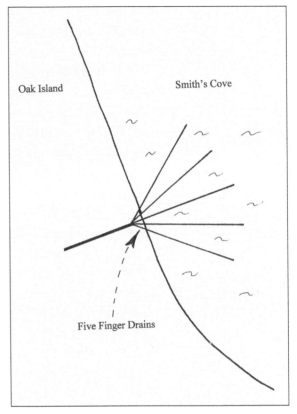

Figure 7: *Under the water at Smith's Cove, the Truro Company found five drains, or conduits, that came together to form a wider drain that travelled through the island to the base of the Money Pit. Sea water was drawn into these drains and flooded the Money Pit whenever searchers got close to the treasure.*

received pressure from the inside, so as the water rushed back to the sea, it broke the top of the cofferdam into pieces. Now, once again, the ocean tides could come and go in Smith's Cove freely. The cofferdam that had permitted the Truro crew to study the beach in such detail was gone, and all the original work on the beach that had been opened up to examination now lay buried by sand.

But the company and crew were determined to press on. They decided not to rebuild the cofferdam, but instead opted to cut off the flow of sea water after it left the beach but before it reached the Money Pit. So, they went down to Smith's Cove beach and tried to find the place where the five finger drains came together. They drew an imaginary line between that spot and the Money Pit. Directly under that line they expected to find a tunnel that brought in sea water. They would block that inlet tunnel so that the water could not get through. They chose a spot partway between the beach and the Money Pit and dug down to a depth of 75 feet (Shaft #4). They found nothing.

So they dug another shaft (#5) a little way from the previous one, this one to a depth of 35 feet. Success! Sea water poured into this shaft.

To block the sea water, they drove a wall of tight-fitting logs down into the earth in front of shaft #5. It had no effect, and the water kept flooding the Money Pit. Their efforts had simply created another shaft (#5) that would fill with water that would rise and fall with the tides.

The Truro Company decided to concentrate their efforts back at the Money Pit, so they went back up to the clearing and dug another shaft (#6) quite close to the pit. This one went deeper than any that had been dug before. From the bottom of this shaft they began to dig horizontally, hoping they would connect with the Money Pit.

Their tunnel was three feet by four feet wide, big enough for a crouching workman. The crew had tunnelled 18 feet toward the Money Pit when they stopped for dinner. They were keeping the level of water in the Money Pit

Horse Gins

A horse gin was a piece of equipment that was driven by a horse and was used for raising great weights or pumping water. If you search for "horse gin" on the Internet, you will find some amazing images.

down by using a horse gin (horses on the surface near the pit turned a big wheel, which generated the electricity to run a pump).

Suddenly, they heard a tremendous crash. When they rushed back and looked into the Money Pit, they discovered that the bottom of the pit had sunk out of sight.

One crewmember who had been working in the new tunnel at the time of the crash barely escaped. As he raced to stay ahead of the muddy avalanche, he managed to grab hold of a round piece of wood that resembled a keg-end that was painted yellow.

Looking into their new shaft (#6), the workers could see that the bottom 12 feet was filled with mud and debris. Looking into the Money Pit, they could see farther down than ever before — deeper than the level where their auger went through the casks of a treasure. The treasure had either broken into the tunnel leading from the newest shaft or had fallen into the space under the spruce platforms. Or perhaps it was strewn between both.

Regardless, the bottom of the Money Pit had collapsed and things were no longer where they had always been. This disaster marked the end of the Truro Company, for they, like the Onslow Company before them, had run out of cash.

More of a Mystery than Ever Before

Through the efforts of the three boys, the Onslow Company, and then the Truro Company, it was clear that sometime before 1795, persons unknown had come to Oak Island and carried out incredible work. They created the formation of stone and vegetation that made up a kind of pavement under Smith's Cove beach, with a "reservoir" at its centre. They built the five finger inlet drains underwater in Smith's Cove to draw sea water into the island. They then tunnelled more than 500 feet through the hard clay of the island to connect the five finger drains to the base of the Money Pit so that sea water would burst into the Money Pit and safeguard the treasure. And they had created the Money Pit itself with its many layers of oak logs, earth, coconut fibre, charcoal, putty, and treasure.

The discovery of all this amazing work fanned the lust for gold. Without question, Oak Island must contain riches beyond belief!

Chapter Five

Odds and Ends

The three teenagers, the Onslow Company, and the Truro Company all made amazing discoveries on Oak Island. Many of the groups that came after them also accomplished important work. Although there is not enough space in this book to tell their full stories, here are some highlights from their discoveries that are important in understanding the Oak Island story.

The Cave-In Pit Is Discovered

By the 1800s, some of the land on Oak Island was being used for farming. One day in 1878, Sophia Sellers was plowing a field that lay between the Money Pit and Smith's Cove when the ground suddenly opened up under one of her oxen and it fell into a deep, wide, well-like hole.

Treasure Hunters Timeline
In Appendix A you will find a timeline that charts all the known treasure hunters who have come to Oak Island. You may find it helpful to refer to the timeline while reading this chapter.

Fortunately, Mrs. Sellers' ox was rescued, although it was quite a struggle to get the animal out. Afterward, the hole became known as "The Cave-In Pit." But what had caused this to happen? No one had any idea.

Fifteen years later, Frederick Blair and the Oak Island Treasure Company began their quest for treasure by clearing this pit out. It was found to be seven feet in diameter, 52 feet deep, and had been carved out of hard clay. Pickaxe marks could clearly be seen in the clay, and the earth within the hole was loose, indicating that it had been dug out before. The pickaxe marks and loose earth were indications that that this pit was part of the original work of the pirates. But its purpose is unclear. Some believe it might have been an air vent for the original underground workers.

The Money Pit

All of the treasure hunters who came to Oak Island had a try at the Money Pit, but it was Frederick Blair and his Oak Island Treasure Company (1893–99) who made the most significant new discoveries.

The Search for Proof

Frederick Blair wanted to be sure that the vault material was cement and not natural limestone. He sent a sample for analysis to a highly-respected laboratory in England. He did not tell them where the sample came from or any other details. The lab reported that the sample was manmade cement, comprised of lime, carbonate, silica, iron and alumina, moisture, and magnesium.

• As they dug down in the Money Pit, at the 111-foot level, they found the entrance to the sea water inlet tunnel. The tunnel was two and a half feet wide and four feet high, and was filled with boulders twice the size of a man's head, which were likely meant to keep the tunnel from collapsing. At the entrance to the tunnel they found a chip of wood, a piece of bark, and a bird bone, which confirmed in their minds that this tunnel was connected to the seashore.

- To their surprise, when they drilled farther down into the Money Pit, water flooded in. This made them ask, "Could there be a second sea water inlet system?" They proved there was by pumping red dye into the Money Pit; it bubbled up in three places on the south shore.

- Boring even deeper in the pit, their drill passed through some cement and then oak. During this exploration their auger brought up a tiny piece of parchment on which was written the Roman numerals *VI* in script. These findings led them to believe that there was a second treasure in the Money Pit. Years before, casks of treasure had been drilled through, and now, at a deeper level, there appeared to be a vault made of cement. They imagined it was filled with gold, jewels, and precious documents. They were stopped from going deeper by a plate of iron.

  Actually, something else was also discovered at that time, but was kept secret. William Chappell was the drill operator who brought up the piece of parchment. Years later he told people that around the time that the parchment was retrieved, he had brought up traces of gold on his drill bit, but he had wiped it off and said nothing. Many years later he formed his own company to search for

Figure 8: This sketch combines all that was believed to have been true about the Money Pit before the Restall family came to Oak Island.

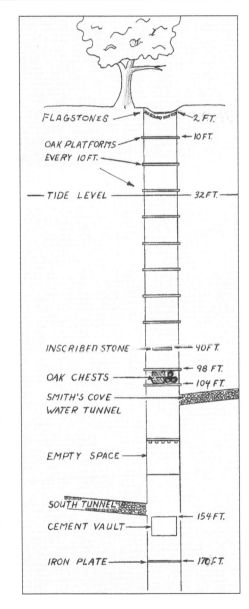

the treasure on Oak Island. Like so many before him, he spent a fortune, but gained nothing.

Oak Island: Fraud or Hoax?

American engineer Captain Henry Bowdoin headed up a search for treasure on Oak Island in 1909. Among his wealthy investors was a young man who would later become president of the United States, Franklin Delano Roosevelt.

Captain Bowdoin told potential investors details of his planned work: he would bring an orange-peel digger (a large earthmover), a crew of men, and an underwater diver to the island. He would drill bore holes to locate the treasure and the inlet tunnel, and then would put down sheet piling to stop the flow of water. He would use the orange-peel bucket to dig up the inlet tunnel from the sheet piling to the shore and then to dig the inlet tunnel from the sheet piling to the Money Pit. After that, the digger would be used to excavate the pit. The crew would use a pump capable of removing water at the rate of 1,000 gallons per minute. If the water was still a problem, he would bring in an air-lock caisson with underwater divers.

Surely, this was the most ambitious plan ever considered for Oak Island.

But when Bowdoin arrived on the island, he seemed to forget his plan. He did nothing to locate the inlet tunnel or to stop the water. He used no sheet piling. He went straight to the Money Pit and pumped it out. He could see that it contained solid platforms every 10 feet that were connected by ladders. These had been left by the last treasure hunter and could have been used by Bowdoin.

But, instead, with his orange-peel digger, Bowdoin ripped out cross-beams, platforms, and ladders down to a depth of 107 feet, stripping the Money Pit bare.

He then built a platform deep in the Money Pit and drilled out at different angles. But he found no sign of treasure, although his drill did go through six inches of cement. *Could that have been the cement vault?*

Frederick Blair controlled the rights to dig for treasure on the island at that time, and he was determined to allow only search parties who could afford to see the job through to its end. When Bowdoin's contract with Blair ran out, and he asked for an extension, Blair asked for proof that Bowdoin had enough money to continue.

> ### Caissons
>
> A "caisson" is a watertight structure within which construction work, such as the assembly of bridge foundations, is carried out underwater. A concrete structure is built around the work area. In an air-lock caisson, water is kept out and fresh air for the workers is pumped in.

Bowdoin replied that if he was not given an extension, he would be forced to write an unfavourable report about Oak Island. Blair remarked that this sounded like a threat, and repeated his request for proof the Bowdoin could finance further work.

But Bowdoin did not provide proof. Instead, he wrote an article, published in *Collier's Magazine*, New York, entitled "Solving the Mystery of Oak Island." In it he stated that there was not and never had been a treasure on Oak Island. He listed his reasons. (As an example, one reason offered was that there could not be an underground sea water tunnel because the distance was too great.)

Blair replied to this article in a Nova Scotia newspaper, the *Amherst Daily News*, giving reasons why Bowdoin was wrong on each point he had made, and adding that Bowdoin had not explained things known to be true about Oak Island; for example, the five-finger drain work in Smith's Cove. Blair concluded by accusing Bowdoin of damaging the island and destroying the Money Pit for no reason at all.

And that was the end of Captain Henry Bowdoin's treasure hunt on Oak Island. He was the first, but not the last, to call Oak Island a fraud.

The Stone Triangle

In 1897, along the south shore of the island, a formation of stones had been found hidden among the bushes and trees. The stones were laid out in the shape of a triangle. Their purpose was not known. When a later searcher, Gilbert Hedden, rediscovered the stone formation, he realized that it was very similar to a sailor's sextant. A sextant is a triangular tool used since ancient times to navigate the sea. By pointing the sextant at the North Star and noting the horizon, a sailor can determine his location on a ship's chart. Hedden discovered that in the stone formation on Oak Island, the head stone (or "pointer" on a sextant) pointed exactly due north to the Money Pit.

On the back cover of this book, you will find a rare photograph of the stone triangle, as it appeared when the Restall family came to the island.

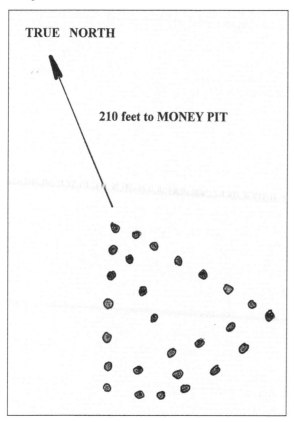

Figure 9: The Stone Triangle or Sextant.

TRUE NORTH

210 feet to MONEY PIT

Destruction and Safety

By the time my family came to Oak Island, many treasure-hunting groups had come and gone. After the original Money Pit was discovered, more than 21 deep shafts and even more tunnels had been burrowed into the island. With each of those shafts and tunnels, sea water had flooded in and been pumped out, again and again. Think erosion.

Each searcher had to deal with oozing mud, sliding cribbing, and collapsing tunnels as a result of work that had gone before. Through the years, the exact location of the Money Pit was lost and found, then lost and found again among the maze of underground tunnels and shafts. More than once the hunters thought they were digging in the Money Pit, only to discover that they were actually working in a previous searcher's shaft.

Often there would be no activity on the island for years. At times, no one had the money to undertake anything as frivolous as a treasure hunt. During those periods of inactivity, the surface of the island had a chance to heal, although the underground maze remained.

The Curse of Oak Island

Many people believe that Oak Island is cursed.

By the time the Restalls arrived to search for the treasure, two treasure hunters had already died on Oak Island.

In 1861, pumps that ran on steam power had been brought to the island, but when one of the boilers burst, a workman was scalded to death and several others were injured. Sadly, we do not know the name of the man who was the first to lose his life in search of the treasure on Oak Island.

In 1897, while the Oak Island Treasure Company hunted for treasure, working crewmember Maynard Kaizer was being raised by a pulley in one of the shafts when the rope slipped from the pulley and he fell to his death.

Before 1795, Oak Island had long been the subject of ghost stories. Mysterious fires reportedly appeared on the island at night, and it was said that men who rowed out to investigate never returned.

Of the many treasure hunters who came to the island after 1795, each encountered machinery breakdowns, weather that seemed to conspire against them, and endless delays, obstacles, and bad luck. Some who began their search as rich men ended it penniless.

> ## Chappell's Pond
> *Over the years, the large hole referred to as "Chappell's Pond" filled with freshwater. Later, my family would find it to be a great source of drinking water. It made a good ice-skating rink for Ricky, too!*

As an example of the uncanny mishaps that occurred on Oak Island, Mel Chappell and Frederick Blair formed a partnership to search for the Oak Island treasure in 1951. They arranged for a huge clamshell digger to be brought to the island. In true Oak Island style, their digger slipped off the barge and sank in Mahone Bay. They brought over another to replace it and, with the help of new radar technology, they claimed they were able to pinpoint the exact location of the treasure. They began to dig, but once the hole was very large, the radar showed that the treasure was no longer there but was located some distance away. Blair and Chappell came to the conclusion that the new radar technology was useless on Oak Island and gave up. The large area they had excavated later became known as Chappell's Pond.

Some people believe that all those occurrences prove that an evil spirit inhabits Oak Island — a spirit that will stop at nothing to safeguard its treasure.

Lucky are the ones who lose only their money.

Chapter Six

So This Is Oak Island

The day after arriving on the east coast, my father, mother, and Bobby headed across the water to Oak Island, where they docked at Hedden's Wharf in Smith's Cove (see Figure 1, page 15). Local boatmen had kept the wharf in good repair since Gilbert Hedden had ended his search for treasure on the island in 1934.

After they landed, my family trudged across the beach and up a hill to the highest part of the island, a large, flat clearing bordered by evergreen trees. Near the far side of the expanse they saw two large, rectangular holes with weather-worn cribbing poking out at the surface — the Money Pit!

The first shaft had been dug by William Chappell in 1931 through hard clay on one side and loose earth on the other, which led it to be badly twisted. By the time the Restalls arrived, it was seriously deteriorating. Beside Chappell's shaft was a larger shaft (Shaft #22), which was wide, deep, and straight. It had been dug by Gilbert Hedden in 1932. These two shafts covered the site of the original Money Pit.

After they had taken a long look, the family decided to explore more of the island. Just a few steps away they found a huge excavation filled with water. This was Chappell's Pond.

Just past the Money Pit, the land dropped quite steeply to the south shore. They descended and made their way along the beach, then turned inland to follow the edge of a swamp that seemed to cut the island in two. They then turned left and walked down the forested middle of the island, past a series of stone fences that marked the location of long-abandoned farms. At the far end of the island, quite close to the mainland, they found an old white wood farmhouse in a state of collapse. They turned, and headed back.

My mother, writing in her journal about that day, compared the condition of the Money Pit to what it had been four years earlier when, during a vacation, she had thought that Oak Island was just an interesting side trip. She had no idea that Dad was hoping to be the next Oak Island treasure hunter.

On October 15, 1959, the day after we arrived at Western Shore, we rented a boat to get over to the island. It was a raw, windy day and by the time we reached the dock, my husband closed the throttle with a firm twist. It snapped clean off. "That's a good start," I thought. An omen? Well we were here, so off we went to see the pits.

"The Pits"

Sometimes my parents referred to the two shafts as "the pits," sometimes as "the Money Pit," and sometimes by their individual names — "the Hedden Shaft" and "the Chappell Shaft."

It had been four years since I last saw the pits, and standing there looking down at them I was shocked at their condition. One pit had partially collapsed, leaving broken and twisted timbers around; you could no longer see the water (at the bottom of the pit). In the other, the larger of the two, rotting cribbing was visible, as all the deck planking had been ripped off, exposing it to the weather. Even my son's face fell momentarily. Looking across the slate grey sea at the black smudges of other islands, I felt utterly wretched. I don't think I have ever seen a place so bleak and lonely as that island, that day. I just wanted to go home.

Soon Bobby's eyes began to sparkle as he and his dad walked around, talking. They walked here, they walked there, son asking questions, my husband answering … all about the history of the place. I trailed after them, ignored and unnoticed. Finally Bob said it was time for us to go back. Catching sight of my face with its woebegone expression, he started to laugh, "Look," he said to Bobby, pointing to me, "The reluctant treasure hunter." They both thought that was hilarious and went off down the hill, roaring with laughter.

Back in the boat, Dad, Mom, and Bobby headed across the bay toward the mainland.

The next day, bright and early, they bought some lumber, and then loaded the lumber, tools, and a few other belongings into the boat and headed for the island.

Their first task was to build a shack beside the Money Pit where they could store the equipment. The shack they constructed was eight feet by 12 feet, and when it was completed, they separated the tools and other items to be left on the island, set them inside the shack, padlocked the door, and pointed their boat toward the mainland.

For the next two days a storm raged, holding them captive on the mainland. Their 15-foot outboard motorboat would have been no match for the towering waves and churning sea.

Mildred Restall stands in front of "the shack," the family's first Oak Island home, October 1959. In the foreground are "the pits"—William Chappell's Shaft and Gilbert Hedden's Shaft. They were dug on the site of the original Money Pit.

When the weather finally cleared and they could get back to the island, they found that someone had broken into the shack. Gone were blankets, tools, and equipment worth about $200.

That was it. No more construction shack, no more motel, no more braving the sea to go back and forth daily to the mainland. They cut windows into the front and back of the shack, bought a propane heater and a camp stove, and moved all their belongings to the island — the shack became their home.

Now, before we go any farther, let's just be sure we're on the same page — there was no electricity on the island. They had to use a propane stove and heater, naphtha lamps to read by, and a battery-driven car radio to listen to the news once a week. Eventually they acquired a few gasoline engines to keep a bank of batteries constantly charged — to run the winch and to do countless other small jobs.

Also, there was no telephone on the island. To make a call they had to take the boat to a dock on the mainland, walk to their car, drive to a nearby gas station, place the call at the payphone, and hope that the person they were trying to contact was home to answer. If there was a call coming in for them, they had to arrange to be at the payphone at a specific time, and then hope that the sea wouldn't be too rough for them to cross. Many times it was. Other times they made arrangements to be there, but had to wait and wait at the payphone for a call that either came late or didn't come at all.

They had no refrigerator, and had to survive on canned meats, powdered milk, and other non-perishable foods. They were able to get fresh meat on food shopping days, which involved a trip to the mainland, a walk to the car, then a 15-minute drive to the town of Chester and the Shamrock Food Store, which sold a range of goods and allowed them to "buy now and pay later," as the local fisherman did. Two short blocks away from the Shamrock was the post office, where they received their mail.

At the beginning, drinking water had to be purchased, but later they had the water from Chappell's Pond tested. It was fine. After that the water was pulled, by the bucketful, from the pond and poured through layers of cheesecloth to, as my mother said, "screen the bugs out." Then it was boiled. It was delicious.

Bath water required carrying many more buckets of water. The toilet was a "privy" or outhouse.

Their new home resembled a rustic summer cabin that had been pressed into year-round service.

Chapter Seven

An October Start?

Starting a treasure hunt in the month of October may seem a bit strange. It was Canada and, as we all know, the winters are cold. The ground freezes. But there were good reasons to start the hunt in October.

Time and again, searchers had come to Oak Island in late spring, worked through the summer, and packed up and gone home as cold weather closed in. This meant a short season for the search. Years had gone by quickly, without results.

In October 1959, the island was owned by Mel Chappell. He also held the licence (granted through the Treasure Trove Act) to dig for treasure on his property. Only he could say who would be allowed to come to the island and search for treasure. He chose my father for several reasons.

At that time, only a few people were willing to risk their money, time, and energy to dig for treasure on an island where so many had tried over the years, but where no treasure had ever been found. Mr. Chappell had already had some bad experiences with treasure hunters. Everyone declared that he was "the one to bring up the treasure." But when given their chance, they did not work as hard or as long, or spend as much money as Mr. Chappell had expected. Who should Mr. Chappell trust? Why not a plumbing contractor from Hamilton?

And then there was the fact that both Mr. Chappell and his father, William Chappell, had searched for the treasure themselves. Each had put in tremendous effort and spent a small fortune. Each had failed. Mel's father was gone by that time, and Mel himself was in his seventies. Before his time ran out, it was extremely important to him to be able to prove that the treasure of Oak Island existed.

Then along came my dad, who seemed to be (and was) an honest man, and one who possessed technical expertise, knowledge about the island and its history, confidence that he knew how to get the treasure, and the intention to carry out his work without destroying the island. Also, he was a man who would stay on the island *through the winter.*

Starting up in October would be difficult, but my family knew that if they didn't jump the moment they were given the chance, Mr. Chappell would find someone who would. Anyway, by starting in October, they would have several weeks to dig on the beach, set up camp, hunker down for the winter, and be ready for the big push when spring arrived.

Dad believed that one thinking man, working with care, would, in a matter of just months, be able to unlock the secrets of Oak Island and succeed where others, with huge amounts of money and brute force, had failed. Of course, my dad believed he was that "one thinking man."

Although Dad's contract was only for a few months, Mr. Chappell had promised to extend it as soon as he saw progress being made. "No problem," Dad assured the family. "No long-term contracts needed. By next summer, the treasure will be ours."

And so they set to work.

Dad and Bobby examined the Hedden Shaft. It appeared to be in excellent condition, even after all those years. They built a hoist so they could lower and raise equipment in the shaft. It was not long before it was also pressed into service as a refrigerator, since the Hedden Shaft was very cool just above sea water level.

Hoist setup at the Money Pit.

The hoist doubled as the family refrigerator. Photo by Louis Jaques.

Once that was done, they turned their attention the Smith's Cove beach. The plan was to locate the sea water inlet tunnel and block it off. After that, they could take their time working down in the Money Pit (the Hedden Shaft) without the hazard of water pouring in.

They began by digging a series of test holes on the beach. Here they came across acorns and oak branches (oaks no longer grew at this end of the island) and great amounts of coconut fibre. Those signs of "original work" encouraged them.

Sometimes they would dig all day, but the next morning would find that rainwater had completely filled the hole overnight. So they would pump out the hole with a small gasoline-driven pump, and keep digging.

Bobby, digging a new beach hole, 1959. The caption in his photograph album reads, "Reaching stone and vegetation layer."

Mildred Restall stands beside the first cribbed hole. Cribbing is cut from island trees.

They would often spend days digging a deep hole without finding any sign of the sea water inlet tunnel. They would then move to another spot on the beach and start the process again.

In November, Mom wrote that it rained almost every day, but that the "men" (Dad and 18-year-old Bobby) continued to work. She described the cramped living space in the shack, and how she had to paw her way through the wet work clothes that hung from the rafters. The clothes seldom completely dried, and many times had to be put back on while they were still damp; the smell of mould filled the shack.

My mother's heart ached for city life. While the men worked away on the beach, she did her best to explore the island and enjoy nature, but she was homesick. Wisely, I think, my father convinced her to return to Hamilton to be with Ricky, who had stayed with me in Ontario to attend school. She would return to the island with Ricky after school finished at the end of June.

On December 21, my parents set out for Hamilton, Dad having hitched his empty box trailer to the car so that he could bring equipment and supplies back with him.

For five weeks, Bobby was left alone on the island to guard their belongings and equipment. My mother never mentioned it without looking a little ashamed — just 18 and all alone on the island. But now I realize that this must have been the moment when Bobby first went to the mainland alone and met other teenagers from the town of Western Shore.

My dad was convinced that the family would be on the island for less than a year, and he intended, during that time, to work every daylight hour, seven days a week. He expected Bobby to do the same, but Mom stepped in and said no, it was too much. Dad didn't give up easily, but finally agreed to let Bobby have time off on Saturday nights. Soon they changed that to include Sunday mornings as well, because they didn't want him rowing back to the island in the middle of the night. He was to be back on Sundays, ready to work by noon.

During those small windows of time, Bobby managed to establish a sliver of a life that had nothing to do with Oak Island. He developed lasting friendships and had great times with his new Western Shore friends.

Chapter Eight

And So to Work

Dad returned to the island from Hamilton loaded down with so much equipment in the old car and trailer that he had four blowouts on the way back.

Mr. Chappell had extended Dad's contract to work on the island to the end of 1960. Under the Treasure Trove Act, if the treasure was located, the government of Nova Scotia would get five percent of anything found. The contract between Dad and Mr. Chappell was an agreement that after the government received its share, the rest of the treasure would be divided equally between the two of them.

Now that he had a contract for a year, Dad was able to take in investment money from other parties. But Dad only wanted one financial partner — his long-time friend and fellow plumbing contractor, Fred Sparham, who came in for 25 percent of Dad's share of the treasure.

The search couldn't have gone ahead without Fred's money, but Fred was more than investor, he was a friend who was keenly interested in everything that was happening on Oak Island.

To keep Fred up-to-date, Dad wrote him long letters. Calls from the payphone were too hard to arrange, and too costly — save for emergencies.

In February, Dad wrote to Fred telling him about the difficulties they faced on the island during the winter months:

> We are getting a bit of work done, but this storm, the biggest ever here beating the record 1894 snowstorm, just can't be overcome.... Just to get to the Mainland and get food and back takes best part of a day. The only good points are that we have no help to pay, and that Mildred is staying in Hamilton at least till the middle of March. We will have to keep the outboard out of the water for a month yet. There is about 24" of frost in the ground. The ice is quite solid in the bottom of the excavation [their last beach hole] but an air hammer with a spade will chew it up fast. [They would soon bring a compressor to the island]

To get to the mainland at that time, Bobby and Dad had to trudge the full length of the island in deep snow, dig out a skiff they kept there, row over to the mainland, then make their way up to the car and dig it out. Many times they then had to dig out the entire street to get to the highway.

And surviving those long nights on Oak Island in that flimsy shack must have been a special test of endurance. Neither Dad nor Bob ever spoke of it. When asked, Bobby would only shake his head and say, "It was grim."

Storm after storm battered the island that February. At the end of the month, Dad wrote to Fred Sparham again. In it, he talked about the work that Bobby and he had been able to accomplish. They had built a float for the boat so that they could put it in and out of the water quickly, and the weather had improved enough that week that they were able to launch the boat. They had nearly finished building the frame for the hoist to be used for removing the earth they dug out of the holes in the beach, and had pumped out the last beach hole and dug out the snow and ice, ready to set a hoist in.

They also attached the gasoline motor, the transmission, and the hoist together in one single unit so that they could use it to pull the boat in or out of the water and then move it over to lift the earth out of the hole. Once they located the inlet tunnel, they planned to pump cement into the hole to clog the five finger drains and stop the sea water from coming into the Money Pit. Then they could finally go after the treasure.

Bobby had been daddy's little helper since he was around four years old — fascinated by all things mechanical. In high school, he had been a shop ace. So he was the perfect person to be working alongside Dad. Whether it was digging for treasure or merely trying to survive, Oak Island was all about mechanics.

In Dad's letter to Fred Sparham in early March, he told him that he had been able to purchase a pump for the Money Pit that had been used by an earlier treasure hunter, Professor Edwin Hamilton. As soon as the weather improved, they would rent a heavy-duty barge and bring the big pump over to the island. Then they'd be able to pump out the Money Pit and go after the treasure.

In that March letter, Dad described the day when a group of local fishermen paid a visit to the island. He had shown them the shaft that he and Bobby were digging on the beach at Smith's Cove. The fishermen had heard all the stories about searching for treasure on the island, but they had never seen proof of anything worth digging for. Now, looking down into the shaft, they could clearly see the layers of stone, sand, and coconut fibre. They were amazed. Each of them left the island that day with a small souvenir bundle of coconut fibre and a broad smile on his face.

A look into the "original" beach work. Layers of stones, vegetation, and clay could be seen in beach "pavement" created by the pirates.

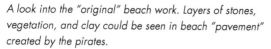

The '47 Plymouth arrives on the island.

Bobby thought that a record should be kept of all their work, so he bought a child's lined scribbler and wrote his first journal entry on March 20. From that day on, he made an entry for every day that they were on the island.

They decided it would be a good idea to have a car and a compressor on the island. With the compressor they would be able to dig through the frozen ground and hard clay, and the car would allow them to ferry heavy equipment and supplies from beach level up to the clearing 32 feet above it.

Bobby's second journal entry, March 21, described building a raft by using lumber and empty 50-gallon drums. When they tested it out, Bobby recorded that it was like an iceberg — two-thirds of it was underwater. To keep the 5,000-pound (2,268-kilogram) compressor above water, they had to add another eight drums to the 12 already attached to the raft's underside. But eventually they managed to get both items over to the island.

On April 8, Bobby turned 19. For the rest of that month and well into May, he and Dad concentrated on searching for the inlet tunnel at the beach at Smith's Cove.

As they dug, again and again they came across signs that they were not the first — a post here, a wooden box there, very old boards from a small retaining wall, and uniform layers of flat stones, sand, eel grass, and coconut fibre. Each find was examined with great care. They needed to know whether each was "original work" or just evidence of previous treasure hunters.

Whenever they found themselves in a spot that had never been dug before, they moved on. They wanted to dig in earth that had been dug before, preferably only by the pirates.

The compressor crosses Mahone Bay on its way to the island.

Some of the earth they encountered was a formless, oozy mess that seeped through their cribbing. This led them to experiment with a number of different methods of construction. On the outside, they would usually place tree poles they had cut on the island and nailed together (known as "spiles"). Inside that they nailed horizontal or vertical boards, or both, one inside the other. Usually they would dig and hammer the cribbing down as they went. On at least one occasion they dug down to the clay layer in open-pit style, then placed the pre-built cribbing into the hole and continued down from there.

Their beach hoist and dump bucket system was run by a small gasoline engine, and the contraption moved the earth up and out of the new beach shaft and deposited it in the cove, where the tides carried it away.

The beach shaft with horizontal and vertical cribbing. The roof had been borrowed from their tent-trailer to keep rain and snow off the work.

Open pit with cribbing ready to go in.

Work was slow because they had to dig with care and inspect everything. Mechanical breakdowns were frequent, and many times they had to stop work and make a quick trip to the machine shop on the mainland to make a repair or to hone a new part. But they pressed on. Slow or not, hole by hole, they were gaining a clear understanding of the pirates' work at Smith's Cove beach.

Near the end of May it was necessary to turn their attention away from the beach and focus on the Money Pit. Soon the pump would arrive on the island. When Professor Hamilton had used it, the pump had been able to remove 450 gallons (2,047.5 litres) of water per minute from the Money Pit. It was immense and very heavy, but it would get rid of the sea water while Dad and Bobby went after the treasure.

Pump strainer and impellers go in.

The completed A-frame. Tourists were ever-present to inspect the work.

In preparation for receiving the pump, they set to work building a "bridge" or A-frame over Hedden's Shaft so that the weight of the huge pump would not have to rest on the disintegrating timbers at the top of the old shaft.

Bobby's journal records cutting down trees, stripping them, then either hauling them across the island or transporting them by the boat-float to Smith's Cove. They also brought milled lumber from the mainland to the beach. Then, using the car, and with some hired help, materials were transported up the hill to the Money Pit, where they would form part of the A-frame. Bobby's journal entries reveal a steady grind of hard, physical labour.

Chapter Nine

Summer in Paradise

On June 21, Ricky and Mom arrived on the island after their long journey from Hamilton to Halifax by train.

My mother believed that they would be there only for the summer, because, as Dad had said, it would only be a short time before the treasure was up, and then they could be on their way. Mom pushed aside any bad memories from the previous October and November — Oak Island could be endured for a few months. But to her amazement, she fell in love with Oak Island that summer. She wrote:

> What a difference. The island was a riot of colour. The magnificent firs a rich green. The grass a thick carpet. And up in the clear, blue sky, the sun shone bright and golden. Sailboats were gliding over a sparkling sea and small craft skimmed around the bay. The air was fragrant with the perfume of wild roses that grew in abundance all over the island. Standing on the beach and looking out over Mahone Bay, with emerald

islands dotted here and there, I thought that never, anywhere, had I seen a place more beautiful.

Mom and Ricky set about happily exploring their new paradise. Daily observations on these jaunts included a beaver family, foxes, numerous small red squirrels, a variety of birds, and the endless moods of the sea. Each day's excursion brought fresh discoveries.

And Ricky, now nine years old, also enjoyed some adventure time alone. He became very good at rowing the skiff, and countless hours were spent manoeuvring the tiny boat through the waters near Smith's Cove. And day in and day out, he swam inside the cofferdam.

One Sunday, a couple of scuba divers from New Jersey came to the island. Rick hovered about, watching them closely, and eventually they took a few minutes to teach him the art of snorkelling. Later, the divers shared their bounty with the family. Everyone squeezed into the tiny shack, feasting on freshly caught flounder and drinking tea. Before the divers left, they gave Ricky a mask and snorkel — a thoughtful gift that gave him lasting passage into the wonders of the underwater world.

My family was astonished by the number of visitors who came to the island. Through the week, local boatmen would bring small groups over to see the famous island. Sometime these men acted as guides, walking the tourists up to the Money Pit, explaining all that had gone before. At other times they just left the tourists on the island and returned for them an hour or so later.

On Sundays, even more visitors came to the island, not only tourists, but also many locals who came in their own motorboats or sailing vessels. All day, clutches of moored boats bobbed up and down in the water just beyond Hedden's Wharf. Visitors toured the worksites, spread their picnic lunches on the beach, and stayed for the day. There was a kind of joyous, carnival spirit to it all.

The brigantine Albatross, an American floating classroom.

The Albatross

Nothing in the visit by the Albatross foretold the tragedy that would occur just nine months later. As the ship was on her way to Florida on May 2, 1961, she was suddenly struck by a "white squall" — an unpredictably sudden, very strong windstorm. The ship keeled over and sank almost immediately, taking with her the ship's doctor, the cook, and four young students.

Bobby and Dad found that all this activity interfered with work, however. Tools, equipment, and the shacks had to be locked up at all times and extra log fencing and chicken wire had to be strung up to keep visitors from falling into the pits. And as Dad and Bobby laboured away, they often found a visitor right at their elbow trying to pull them aside for a private Oak Island history lesson.

Mom and Ricky had to fend off these strangers, too. But once in a while a visitor would arrive who already knew a lot about Oak Island and was fascinated by the work going on. My mother and dad enjoyed spending some time with visitors such as these.

On August 14, the brigantine *Albatross* moored out in the cove. She was an American ship, serving as a floating classroom for students taking preparatory college courses and sail-training. That day, along with their captain, a group of the students rowed out to the island to take a tour of the site and observe the work that was going on.

That evening some of the students returned to the island. This time they ferried my mother and father to the *Albatross* for a shipboard dinner, returning them to the island just before nightfall. My mother said it was a charming evening. The next day, the *Albatross* and her crew were on their way south.

When my mother and Ricky had arrived on the island near the end of June, the A-frame over the Money Pit was almost finished and the parts for the pump had arrived on the island. But it was July 18 before the pump was assembled and ready for a test run. A sigh of relief was heard as the massive pump rumbled into action and slowly emptied the Money Pit.

On July 25, Dad wrote to Fred Sparham to let him know that the big pump had proved it was capable of removing water from the Money Pit faster than it came in, but that it had taken three days of pumping and six barrels of gas to empty it. Starting and stopping the pump would be inefficient and costly, but keeping the pump running night and day was no better. Working in the Money Pit was going to be very expensive.

Around the same time, my mother wrote to me. She mentioned that it was fine to leave the tunnels and shafts full of sea water, as they had been for years, because water in the shafts kept a constant pressure on the old timbers. If the water was pumped out, that old wood might not be strong enough to withstand a collapse. It sounded terrifying to me.

If only Dad and Bobby could find the sea water inlet tunnel down on the beach, they would not have the ruinous expense of running the pump night and day, they would not have the rush of water in and out eroding the earth underground, and they could take whatever time they needed for careful inspections and repairs to shafts and tunnels before beginning their own underground work.

They *had* to find the sea water inlet.

All summer, whenever they could not work in the Money Pit, they went back to work on the beach. Again and again they uncovered evidence of the pirates' work.

Mildred Restall washing off stones dug out of the "reservoir."

In October, they were certain they had located the edges and the centre of the pirates' work on the beach. The work covered far more ground than anyone had previously thought. The reservoir lay in the centre of the beach work and occupied about one-third of the total area. At the very centre of the reservoir they found sand lying in varying layers of coarseness. In time they would come to realize that the reservoir acted not only as a sponge to hold water, but also as a filter to keep sand out of the sea water inlet tunnel. As it was filtered out, the sand formed layers.

Around the reservoir was a ring of stones that seemed to act as a seal. One of the stones in the ring had the date 1704 carved in it.

Various types of stone formations were found in other parts of the beach work. As an example, Bobby noted in his journal that when he was putting cribbing into the new hole, he came across a number of rocks: "Nearly all the rocks were placed in with the long way down or on end and tightly packed in." In other words, it seemed as if someone had carefully placed the stones there in a specific way.

For Bobby and my dad, these discoveries confirmed that they were on the right track and helped guide them as they moved ahead with the project.

Let's talk about the 1704 stone. As I mentioned before, by using the dump bucket system, Dad and Bobby deposited the soil and stones taken from all their diggings on the beach into the waters of Smith's Cove, where they would be washed away by the tides. Even today, Rick clearly recalls that day on the beach. It was November 6, and the men were digging to expose part of the reservoir while he and Mom were taking one of their usual strolls around the island. During their explorations, they decided to walk over and take a closer look at the pile of stones that had recently been deposited by the dump bucket. When Mom thought she saw some kind of marking on one of the discarded stones, she sent Ricky to get Bobby and his dad.

At first a bit grumpy to be called away from their "real" work, the men reluctantly followed Ricky over, took a look, and agreed that it appeared there was something written on the stone. They were not sure what it was, but decided to carry it up to the shack for closer inspection. There it sat for months; but as the stone dried out, little by little the carving became more and more legible, until at last it could clearly be seen that this small, heavy, olive-coloured stone was deeply carved with the numbers *1-7-0-4*.

Ricky holding the 1704 stone found in reservoir section of the pirates' beach work. Photo by Louis Jaques.

Chapter Ten

1704? What Does It Mean?

The 1704 stone had come from a ring of stones near the edge of the "reservoir" in the middle of the beach at Smith's Cove, some three feet underground. This stone fit tightly between stones of a similar size and shape that formed the ring. My father concluded that the ring of stones acted as a seal to keep water inside the central part of the reservoir, providing a "sponge" effect.

Let's pause and think about all the work that would have been going on at the time the treasure was hidden. We are assuming that some unknown persons had a valuable treasure that they wanted to hide on Oak Island. We believe that the Money Pit, Smith Cove's beach work, and a tunnel through the island connecting the two were part of an elaborate plan to safeguard the treasure. How could that have been done?

One scenario is that the men were divided into three work crews. One crew would have stayed up on the clearing to dig out the Money Pit. Down, down, down they dug through the hard clay of the island. When the pit was deep enough, they placed a thick iron plate across the bottom of it. On top of this plate they constructed a cement vault that contained the treasure, including the piece of parchment. Above that they installed the spruce platform. On the platform they placed the three oak casks and two boxes of treasure (where the jewel that reportedly came up on the auger once lay). Above that, another platform of spruce was installed. And then, working their way up and out of the shaft, the crew installed a log platform, putty, coconut fibre, charcoal, and earth, layer after layer. When they were nearly at the surface, they finished with a layer of flat stones covered by a final thin layer of earth.

Like miners boring through a mountain, tracking a vein of gold, a second work crew would have tunnelled through the island to connect the beach at Smith's Cove to the opening, deep down in the Money Pit, so that sea water could flood in and booby-trap the pit.

Down in Smith's Cove, a third crew would have built the cofferdam to hold back the sea, and then would have carefully constructed the five finger drains, the single sea water inlet drain ("wrist"), and then the layers of stones, coconut fibre, and eel grass that lie under the beach sand, including the intricately-layered reservoir that occupies the centre of the beach work.

It's possible that someone on the beach crew carved the date on the stone and set it in place. This carving could not have been done quickly; the stone is very hard, and the cuts are deep.

But why carve a date into a stone? We will never know the answer to that question, but if the carving refers to the year that the treasure was hidden, the date 1704 is quite significant.

Who Put the Treasure on Oak Island?

There are many theories as to who buried the treasure on Oak Island.

From the time the site was first discovered by the three boys — Daniel McInnis, John Smith, and Anthony Vaughan — the theory that pirates were responsible has been the most popular.

Some pirates — the privateers, for example — were educated, skilled men who carried out their piracy on behalf of king, country, or groups of well-connected citizens. But circumstances can be altered; power can change hands. Sometimes privateers found the legal protection under which they sailed had suddenly been revoked and that they were "wanted" men. So they continued their acts of piracy, but now they were working for themselves. My father believed that the men in charge of pirate ships were often intelligent, educated men, quite capable of the elaborate constructions on Oak Island.

If Oak Island's treasure is pirate treasure, the name most often mentioned is Captain William Kidd. But if the 1704 stone represents the year in which the work was done on the island, then Captain Kidd is unlikely to have been part of it, because he was hanged in 1701.

Still, there are many other pirates who might have done this work. Port Royal, Jamaica, a known haven for the vilest of pirates, had suffered a crippling earthquake in 1692, and countless hoards of treasure needed to be relocated to a safer place. Could crews from a number of pirate ships working together have moved the Port Royal treasure to Oak Island?

Sir William Phips, a sea captain from Maine, has lately emerged as a possible suspect. It is thought that while retrieving an enormous treasure in silver from the wreck of the Spanish galleon *Concepcion*, under the sponsorship of the king of England, Phips may have diverted the more valuable part of its cargo to Oak Island. You can read this lively and persuasive argument in *Oak Island and Its Lost Treasure* by Graham Harris and Les MacPhie. However, Phips died in 1695. So this theory is not helped by the 1704 stone either.

Some argue that Marie Antoinette's jewels could be the source of Oak Island's treasure. It is reported that during the French Revolution, Marie Antionette instructed her lady-in-waiting to escape with the jewels. After the Revolution, the lady-in-waiting was sighted in Nova Scotia. According to this theory, the French navy would have been responsible for the underground work on Oak Island. The bulk of Marie Antoinette's jewels have never been found.

Over the years, both Mexico and Spain have issued statements, informally, declaring that the Oak Island treasure is, without question, theirs.

A few people have argued that Oak Island's treasure consists of manuscripts authored by Sir Francis Bacon or William Shakespeare. Others think that the elaborate workings on the island were constructed by the Knights Templar and they believe that Oak Island could be the resting place for the Holy Grail or the Ark of the Covenant.

And it has even been suggested that Oak Island was visited by beings from outer space. According to this theory, the underground work on Oak Island has nothing to do with treasure; it was constructed to provide access to a subterranean control centre in the caverns under the bedrock of Oak Island. It was created by and for the extraterrestials who, in their giant spaceships, roam our ocean beds at their leisure.

Perhaps this would be a good time to discuss treasure maps. Through the years, numerous maps have been linked to Oak Island, but I think one in particular is remarkable.

Gilbert Hedden was searching for treasure on Oak Island in 1937 when a book written by Harold T. Wilkins, *Captain Kidd and His Skeleton Island*, was published in England. It contained a map that supposedly had belonged to Captain Kidd. The map depicted an island that looked suspiciously like Oak Island. When the map and Oak Island were compared, they were found to have some 14 points in common; for example, the general outline of the island was the same, as was the place on the shoreline where boats would have harboured.

The map bore this legend:

18 W and by 7 E on Rock
30 SW. 14 N Tree
7 by 8 by 4

On Oak Island, two hand-drilled white granite stones had been discovered. One had been found by Blair near the Money Pit, and years later another had been found by Hedden near the shore at Smith's Cove. It was believed that they were part of the pirates' original work.

Hedden applied the legend to Oak Island, and when he drew a line between the two granite rocks, they were exactly on an east–west line. When he measured 18 rods west of one rock and 7 rods east of the other rock, he came to the Cave-In Pit. (A rod is an old English country measurement. One rod = 5.0292 metres.) When he drew a line southwest from the Cave-In Pit, and measured 30 rods, he arrived at the stone triangle. From the baseline of the triangle, he measured 14 rods to the north, and found himself at the Money Pit. The measurements on Oak Island fit the legend precisely!

The hand-drilled, white granite stone at Smith's Cove. It had a twin near the Money Pit.

Although no one could figure out what the last line of the legend — "7 by 8 by 4" — corresponded to, the map and its legend caused quite a stir.

When Gilbert Hedden went to England to see this original map and to try to purchase it, he got an unhappy surprise. The author of the book told Hedden that there was no original map. He had drawn the map himself by blending details from several maps he had seen of an island in the

China Sea. He said that the map's legend and measurements had come entirely from his imagination.

Incredible!

While my family was on Oak Island, they located the two granite hand-drilled stones. Dad and Bobby verified for themselves the accuracy of the measurements between the granite stones, the Cave-In Pit, the stone triangle, and the Money Pit, and used the measurements again and again as their base as they tried to determine the logical location for the sea water inlet tunnel or the "walk-in tunnel," which earlier searchers had imagined existed to allow the pirates to retrieve their treasure without triggering their own booby traps.

Through the years there have been countless maps that supposedly had a connection to Oak Island, but none of them proved more helpful than the map that was, from what we've been told, a total fake.

Chapter Eleven

Meanwhile, Back at the Beach

By the end of that summer in 1960, both Mom and Rick had come to love Oak Island. They wanted to be nowhere else and decided that a winter on the island would be fun. What Ricky was going to do about school was a problem, though. Recently, I asked him to tell me about his school experience while on the island, and this is what he wrote:

> Leaving the island every day to attend school was a practical impossibility. Luckily the government had a program for children in remote places, called Correspondence Courses. These were regular courses, modified so that a teacher wouldn't be required, just an adult to help guide the pupil.
>
> After my first summer on the island, having schoolwork appear suddenly in September was a horrible shock. I rebelled as much as I could, by dithering over the work, doodling in the margins, or looking out the window. This rebellion was noted

by my mother, and dealt with. "Take all day if you want," she said cheerily, "the lesson will be done before you can go out to play." Play? With whom? I was the only kid on the entire island! However, it was a vast and unexplored island, with many mysteries I was itching to uncover. There was no way that I could avoid the lessons, or trick Mom into doing them for me — so I buckled down and finished the schoolwork as soon as I could, in an average of three hours per day for grade 4. And Mom did help me as much as she was allowed by educational rules.

Lessons arrived in the monthly package. The lessons for the week were carefully removed and the package resealed, at least in the early years, because there were books in the package intended for my school supervisor (Mom) that helped her to guide my reading, writing, and arithmetic … [they] might give away some answers that I was supposed to arrive at by myself. Once I completed the week's lesson, they were mailed back to the Education Department for marking.

As the years progressed, my schooldays got longer, five or six hours per day by the 8th grade, depending on the weather. If it was nice, I tried to get through as fast as possible. And if it was heavy rain or snow, I dawdled my way through the lessons and then retired to Bobby's cabin, where I read paperbacks like Tarzan and other adventure literature. And by the 8th grade, Mom could only help me with English or History. She had little knowledge of science, geography, or math because she had been forced to leave school at an early age.

"Bobby's Cabin"
Bobby's cabin was the beach shack. Bobby and Ricky used it as their bunkhouse, and although their meals and evening social times were spent in the main shack with my parents, they slept in the beach shack.

Rick with his new pup.

Despite his schoolwork, Ricky continued to enjoy seeking out the wildlife on the island and collecting tiny sea creatures; but soon it was decided that he was ready for something more. He should have a dog.

So in mid-October, when Dad had to go to Halifax on business, Mom and Rick went along to do some "dog-shopping." Apparently, Dad's business matters took much longer than expected, leaving enough time to visit only one place, where they found only one dog.

They had hoped for a dog that would take guarding responsibilities seriously — perhaps a German shepherd — but instead they came back with a black puppy that they were told was a six-week-old Belgian shepherd, but who, as she matured, looked suspiciously like a black lab or a flat-coated retriever. The breeder assured them she would become a great watchdog, but this did not turn out to be the case. Instead, she was everybody's friend. The breeder said she would mature into a medium-sized dog who would eat almost nothing. Really? She ate and she grew. She ate and she grew. Her appetite was alarming.

They named her Carney, after the canned Carnation milk that she so loved. She was a joyful animal who adored Rick. She was the perfect companion for a young boy, and the two roamed the island together, nothing escaping their scrutiny.

As Mom and Rick happily settled in for an idyllic winter on Oak Island, Dad and Bobby had plenty to worry about. Back in August, Mel Chappell had come to the island for a visit with a *National Geographic* photographer. It was a pleasant and cheerful day as Dad showed the two men the ongoing work and accomplishments. During that visit, Chappell mentioned that Dad would be given a contract for another year.

But as winter settled in, it seemed that conversation was forgotten, and my dad was told that the current contract would run out at the end of December (1960). Contract or no contract, Dad and Bobby kept working.

According to Bobby's journal, they continued to dig on the beach every day up until Christmas. There was no work on Christmas Day, but they were back on the beach digging the next day, and they kept at it into the new year.

Fred Sparham's investment money was running out. Dad considered running the pump and working down the Money Pit until the fuel tanks ran dry, but decided against it. He preferred to trust that Mr. Chappell would come through with an extension. And so ended 1960.

At the start of the new year, winter took over. My mother's description of that time is worth reading:

> Winter really came to stay shortly after the New Year, 1961. The thermometer dropped down to zero at nights, often lower. During the day, it never once climbed over 13 degrees for over six weeks. The bay froze solid. Ice began [to form] along the shore, and daily crept out further and further. Every morning after breakfast I hurried down to the beach to see how close the ice was coming to our end of the island. Overnight it advanced fifty, one hundred feet. Finally we were completely icebound. The calm weather and zero temperatures had brought the severest winter in nearly forty years.
>
> It was bitterly cold. We found birds frozen to death, one a great hawk. You could walk through the woods and hear tree branches snap like a pistol shot.
>
> People on the shore skated over to the island. For the first time in living memory for some of the residents, there was ice-

boating. Even cars could be driven over to Oak Island. Some of the younger set took to having car races on the ice. At night it was a sight to see — huge bonfires lit along the shore for skating parties. As far as you could see there were acres and acres of ice.... It was cold, bitterly cold.

The cold penetrated the thin walls of the shack. We had the heater on full blast, but even so I wore my snow boots all day while working around in the cabin. At night we sat on the bed with our feet curled under us; it was too cold near the floor. You froze from the knees down. From the knees up to the shoulders was fine, but the rest of you was too hot for comfort. Now it was too cold to do any laundry outside, so every day I rinsed out a few odds and ends indoors. With daily dishwashing, cooking and laundry, the shack was very humid. This warm, moist air floated up to the ceiling, and as the sun moved off the roof, it froze. Next day, when the sun hit squarely on the shack, this ice would melt. Starting at around 11:00 a.m. it would drip all over the place ... on the bed, floor, even on Ricky's school work. It began to collect around the bottom of the walls and freeze. By the middle of February we had ice an inch or more thick all around the bottom of the walls and up to a height of two feet in some places.

It was so cold that whenever the door was opened, the outside frigid air swept in and collided with the warm, moist air at the open door and there they struggled, a huge cloud of vapour rolling back and forth in the doorway. So cold that when I threw out a pan of dishwater it bounced on the snow.

How we stuck it out, I'll never know. I worried about Ricky, who was susceptible to ear trouble. But in spite of all the miseries of cold, and lack of conveniences, we were as healthy as horses.

Not one of us got even the sniffles.

So there the family was, living in a shack on an island, in the middle of a Canadian winter, with the last of the money slowly leaking away, and with no contract that would allow the Restalls to continue their dig.

Now my father's letters to Fred Sparham made reference to the need to bring in an additional investor to raise another $5,000, to "wrap this job up." But if an investor suspected the situation was desperate, he or she might get greedy. Finding an investor who would not demand too big a piece of the pie would not be easy. Finding an investor to come in when there was no contract would be impossible.

A few local people invested $100 or $200, as did one or two of Dad's family members and a couple of friends from Hamilton, but that just helped with survival. It was not enough to finance real work.

In March, Dad wrote to Sparham telling him that Chappell had given him a guarantee that he could continue until sometime in May. Dad urged Fred to try to find investors.

Fred reached out to his friends, and Dad drove to Hamilton to make a slideshow presentation of his work on the island. This would be the first of many such presentations. But although would-be investors were quite impressed, money was scarce, and they thought long and hard before they coughed up even $100 for the project.

Perhaps this would be a good time to mention two issues that hovered in the background during the time my family was on Oak Island.

It is clear that Mel Chappell really wanted my father to succeed in his quest, yet he did not want to give a long contract to anyone. He was concerned about the risk of having the island tied up with someone who made only a half-hearted effort at the treasure, under the security of a contract. But without a contract, who would invest money in a treasure hunt that could be halted at any moment?

The Restall family were never free of the worry that their contract might end. Each year it seemed that this time they really might not get a renewal. But then they would, and every new year their attempts to raise investment money stalled over this uncertainty.

The second issue was less serious, but still an irritation. A steady stream of people with ideas of how to get the treasure contacted Mr. Chappell. Whenever he visited the island, Mr. Chappell would tell my father about this person or that group who wanted to take over the search. Sometimes he brought them over to the island so they could tell Dad their theories and to let them see Dad's work. But really, their aim was to replace the Restalls. My father tried to be courteous for the sake of good relations with Mr. Chappell, but it was a bitter pill to swallow.

Contract or not, the Restalls kept plugging along, living a spartan existence and working every day ... even through the winter.

The long nights were spent poring over information about Oak Island from the Halifax library and the records of previous searchers, or discussing what they found in their own work as compared to those records. And countless hours were spent writing letters to people who might possibly make a little investment in the work, or to those who had already invested, to keep them up-to-date.

On March 6, Dad wrote a long letter to Fred Sparham. In it he mentioned that he and Bobby had dug some 65 holes on the beach. He went on to describe new discoveries they had made, and ways in which previous knowledge about Oak Island's beach work was inaccurate. With this letter, Dad included a sketch of the reservoir. It was on the right side, in the ring of stones that acted as a seal, that the 1704 stone had been found (see Appendix 2).

Dad also described the winter conditions and how the huge ice floes were smashing the wharf:

The winter here has been terrible, the Ice is breaking up, the pieces floating by are 18" to 20" thick with some over two feet thick. This on salt water yet…. There is a storm on now. Waves are only three to three-and-a-half feet but not close together. This gets the chunks of ice (tons) enough momentum to give things an awful beating.

I am going ashore on foot this afternoon. The other half of the island is in solid ice yet. So, will mail this then. We have to wind this job up fast (its here, we can get it, and we are going to get it) but we can't stand much more of the way we have been living. It's enough to drive anyone out of their mind. Do the best you can and we have got to get enough for eating and stove oil, etc. Best regards to all from all of us.

Yours very truly, Bob

Here is what my mother wrote about that time:

It was well into March before the breakup came. I think everybody we knew was glad to see the end of winter. "Worst winter we have had in years," the natives said. It was certainly the worst for me.

As the ice began to break away from the mainland, it floated past our island. Great slabs, some big enough to put a fair-sized house on, went floating by, and many swirled around the end of our wharf to lodge in the cove. They piled up on the beach where the receding tide left them, making miniature cliffs from four to ten feet high….

Before the men could put the boat into the water, it was necessary to clear away some of the ice that was floating in the

*Bobby moving ice
away from the wharf.*

cove. To the boys, this was great sport. Taking long poles, they jumped from one ice mass to the next until they were nearly at the outer edge. Then pushing with all their might, they forced the ice out to where the current would take it past the island. Often when they got back, they would find ice right back in the path they had cleared, and would have to go through the whole business again. Some of the slabs were nearly three feet thick. Hard work.

Chapter Twelve

The Best Summer Ever

It had been a rough winter and spring, both weather-wise and money-wise. It was clear that the job would go on longer and be more costly than they had first expected. Investors must be found.

Fred Sparham had provided the money to start the project, and many times when Dad needed parts, supplies, or equipment, Fred was the one who would get the money together and send the goods. Sometimes he sent cash from his own pocket to tide the family over with food and fuel expenses. He told his son Eddie, "We can't have Bob and his family going hungry out there. It's twenty bucks for us, and twenty bucks for Bob."

Fred did his best to interest others in Oak Island, but even with Dad's trip to Hamilton to present the slideshow, little money was raised.

The story of Oak Island and its treasure hunters was reported time and again, all over the world, as a "stranger-than-fiction" story. Yet most Canadians had never heard of it. All that was about to change.

In 1961, television crews and newspaper and magazine reporters descended

Lloyd MacInnis (right), television journalist, with Mom, Carney, and CBC's The Gazette crewmember, preparing for interview, April 9, 1961.

on Oak Island to tell the story of the Restall family — "modern-day treasure hunters" who traded the comforts and certainties of civilized life for a primitive, harsh, isolated existence, because they were determined to follow their dream.

The first to come that year was Lloyd MacInnis and his crew from the CBC. They were preparing a one-hour television documentary for *The Gazette*. Dad said they brought enough equipment for a Hollywood movie. It was a long day, but a happy one.

Before my mom had met my dad and become a motorcycle rider, she was a dancer in one of the countless variety shows that criss-crossed England. From the age of 12, she had supported herself in show business. Mom was totally at ease in front of the camera and had a talent for storytelling. Audiences small and large found her stories fascinating, and that summer she had many chances to showcase her skills.

Shortly after the CBC visit, a photographer and reporter came to the island from the *Hamilton Spectator* newspaper. They put together quite a big spread, which appeared in the paper that June.

On July 18, Louis Jaques and Cyril Robinson came to the island to do a piece for the *Weekend Magazine*. Jaques had previously done an article on Mom and Dad and the Globe of Death, so it was like a visit from old friends, and there was lots of laughter.

Somewhere near the end of August, a photographer from the *International Harvester* magazine came to the island and took some excellent photographs. Robert Norwood, a photographer from the *Halifax Chronicle*, came in October, and shortly after that a well-crafted article and some superb photographs appeared in the Halifax newspaper.

My mother loved these celebrity moments, and Dad was hopeful that all this publicity would generate some interest from investors.

In the midst of all this, still working on the beach, Dad and Bobby discovered what they believed was some original work done by the pirates. They called their new find "The Vertical Shaft."

As mentioned earlier, a white granite stone with a hand-drilled hole lay on the beach, and if you drew a line from it to its twin stone at the Money Pit, your line touched the Cave-In Pit. Along that line, but not far from the beach granite stone, Dad and Bobby had begun a meticulous examination of the beach.

Right beside the beach shack that Bobby and Ricky slept in they found, to their great surprise, a small dome of stones. When they removed the dome, they found a narrow shaft that was lined with more stones. It went down 43 feet (13.1 metres) and was about 13 inches (0.33 metres) wide.

Discovery of the Vertical Shaft. Mildred and Ricky are wearing bug gear. Ricky has his hand on the stone dome. Beneath it you can see the hole that they named "the Vertical Shaft." In the foreground is the white, hand-drilled granite stone, a marker stone from the time of the pirates.

Dad and Bobby were elated. Surely this was the spot where the pirates intended to come back and plug the sea water inlet tunnel. Now Dad could pour concrete down the hole and stop the inflow of sea water.

Quickly they arranged for a cement mixer, operator, and materials to be brought to the island. Heavy rains held them up a full day and Dad could barely wait. This was it! This was the moment they had worked so hard for.

But it was not meant to be. The cement did not mix smoothly. After they mixed the cement, sand, and water together to make concrete, they pumped it down into the shaft. But it did not make a seal. They tried for hours to correct the problem, but when air pressure was applied, the seal broke and the concrete blew out and travelled underground and out to sea.

Dad blamed himself for not researching Nova Scotia cement better. He expected it to be the same consistency as in Ontario, but it wasn't. He should have put the dry cement through a sieve before adding the sand and water. He didn't, so their concrete was lumpy and incapable of forming a solid seal. Dad was deeply disappointed.

Shortly after that, in the first week of August, Fred Sparham arrived on the island for a brief visit. A day or two later, I arrived for a nine-week stay along with my husband Doug and our three young children. Doug was there to help with the work and I was there to have a vacation in paradise with my young family. The kids and I spent many days swimming in the water inside the cofferdam, lolling on the beach, and exploring the quiet, tree-lined pathways of the island. One day when my mother and Ricky were with us, we came upon a farmer's garden, now abandoned, that was enclosed by a tall, thick wall of blackberries — millions of them — that fell into our hands at a touch. The five of us picked and feasted for hours.

Meanwhile, Dad brought a drill over to the island and the men tried to intercept the sea water inlet tunnel close to the Vertical Shaft, but this time a little closer to shore. When that failed, they moved the drill inland a short distance and tried again. But they still couldn't locate the inlet tunnel (or drain).

During the first week of October, Doug and I packed up the kids and returned to Hamilton. With so much happening on the island, it was difficult for us to leave.

Bobby's journal indicates that he and Dad then went back to one of their beach shafts, dug a tunnel out from its floor, and set up the drill across the bottom of the tunnel in another attempt to locate the inlet tunnel. But again they were unsuccessful.

At the beginning of December, my husband returned to the island to deliver a diamond drill bit and to help with the work. He stayed until December 20. During his stay he wrote to tell me that the earth around the vertical shaft was "like porridge" — an oozy, formless mess. It was impossible to dig. Much later, it would be learned that this was an extremely important site.

During Doug's stay, Davis Tobias, a potential investor, paid a visit to the island. Mr. Tobias had the kind of money that could see the project to its completion, and he seemed very interested. Hopes were high that an investment deal could be struck.

There was no contract for the next year and Chappell was pressuring Dad to work down the Money Pit. But Dad knew that once the pump was started, there had to be an ample supply of gasoline to keep it running. If David Tobias came on board, all that could happen.

Fred Sparham (left), Bobby and Bob Restall, drilling near the Vertical Shaft.

Chapter Thirteen

More of the Same

The Restalls had learned a lot about surviving on the island, so the winter of 1962 was much easier than the previous one. They placed spruce boughs around the shacks for insulation and as a windbreak, and the buildings remained toasty warm.

They continued to drill beside the Vertical Shaft all through January, but the drill bits had a tough time getting through the stone.

Winter roared in as February arrived and the island was once again ice-bound. That meant that whenever they needed food, mail, equipment, or supplies, they had to walk the length of the island, pulling a toboggan, then trudge across the expanse of ice to the mainland, where their car would need to be dug out.

At first, negotiations between Dad and Chappell and between Dad and David Tobias did not go smoothly, but in February a contract was signed by Mel Chappell and Bob Restall that allowed my dad to continue to search for treasure on Oak Island until the end of 1962. At the same time, Mr. Tobias and my father signed a contract that formalized David Tobias's investment in the Restall dig. David Tobias brought much-needed cash and business savvy to the project.

Dad's trips to Ontario also began to pay off at that time, with a steady trickle of investment money from Fred's business associates and some of Dad's friends and relatives. Most of those investments were small, but every dollar helped, and by mid-March, when the weather broke, Bobby and Dad were able to start drilling again.

Spring brought with it another CBC crew making an Oak Island television documentary. This time is was for the program *20/20*.

In April, Dad and Bobby started up the big pump at the Money Pit. The Truro Company's 75-foot shaft (Shaft #4) and 35-foot shaft (Shaft #5) could still be seen on the island (see Figure 1, page 15). As Dad and Bobby pumped the Money Pit, they saw the water level drop in the two old Truro shafts. This verified there was a connection between them and the Money Pit.

Once the Money Pit and the two Truro shafts had been emptied, Dad and Bob were able to rig ladders and climb inside. At the bottom of Shaft #4 they found a tunnel that ran between the two shafts. The underground ladders and cribbing were still in good condition, even after all those years.

In their own drill holes on the beach they had expected that pumping the Money Pit would produce the sound of water rushing, or they would see a rise and fall of the water level, but nothing of the sort happened. That was a disappointment.

On a job such as this, equipment repairs are a constant requirement. That summer they split their time three ways: digging on the beach, repairing equipment, and preparing for work down in the Money Pit.

They bought an old Austin auto for $45.00 and rigged it to provide power for the hoist in the Money Pit, to run a grinder, and to act as a battery charger that could charge three batteries at once.

High tides and storms washed away their work at the beach time and time again.

Behind Bobby is the badly damaged wharf. This destruction happened whenever a fierce storm hit the beach.

In a letter to Fred Sparham, Dad mentioned the need to replace the deck of the boat: "The mahogany veneer has all peeled and the remaining shreds get in our eyes every time we use it. Also our groceries get wet as the water goes through the deck now just as if it wasn't there."

During their time on the island, high tides, storms, and even hurricanes played havoc with their work and equipment. Several times, Hedden's Wharf was reduced to its stone bed, not a stick of wood remaining.

That summer, American investor Karl Graeser came to the island with his wife. Karl had visited the island alone the previous summer. Now, as he and his wife enjoyed a lengthy tour of the ongoing work, Karl clearly was impressed with the progress.

That evening, the Graesers took my parents out to dinner at the Sword and Anchor in Chester, where Karl bombarded Dad with questions about the current work and earlier searchers' discoveries. Then, for hours, he and Dad enthusiastically explored a variety of theories regarding what it could all mean. In the end, Karl confided that he might be ready to invest in the Restall dig. A few weeks later, he did just that. His substantial investment went a long way toward satisfying the pump's voracious appetite for gasoline.

While the men worked, Rick occupied himself in his usual ways, now accompanied by a fully grown and enthusiastic Carney. And my mother gained a modern convenience — a washing machine that was hooked up to a gasoline engine. Even in the dead of winter, it saw full use.

Mildred was happy to get an outdoor washing machine run by a gasoline engine.

My family and I decided to return to Oak Island that summer for an indefinite stay. We truly believed in Dad's search for the treasure, and he needed the help, so Doug and I locked up his business back in Hamilton and headed for Oak Island with the kids.

But that summer was not like the one before. It rained almost every day and was bitterly cold. We almost froze in the tent-trailer.

And the weather didn't break; it stayed wretched. A severe winter was being forecast, as well, so at the end of September, Dad announced that a new cabin must be built. He and my mother would move into it. The boys would continue to sleep in their beach shack and join Mom and Dad for meals and in the evening hours. Doug and I and our three kids would move into the first shack, the converted tool shed. That tiny building proved to be a cozy, perfect home for us.

That fall, as the men were bringing the boat and trailer ashore with the power winch, an eye on the bow of the boat broke free and imbedded itself in Doug's shin. The impact knocked him off his feet and the cut was deep. At daybreak, Dad and Bobby took Doug to the closest hospital, were he was x-rayed, treated, and sent home. Fortunately, there were no fractures. The wound become infected, however, and for a while Doug could only stand for short periods of time. So he propped himself up and took responsibility for constructing the miles (it seemed) of underground air ducts from plywood. After a couple of weeks, he was back in full form.

The Money Pit and connecting tunnels had to be cleared before underground work could commence.

Picture the work area. You descend in Hedden's Shaft. At a depth of 115 feet you can leave the shaft and walk through Professor Hamilton's curving tunnel. Some distance away this tunnel intersects an old Halifax Company tunnel that takes you farther away from the Hedden Shaft.

To get ready for new work, Dad, Doug, and Bobby had to remove abandoned cribbing, mud, and other debris from the shaft and tunnels. Weakened spots in the cribbing had to be shored up and ladders fastened to the walls of the shaft. Tracks had to be attached, as well, so that a power vice could be installed for underground drilling. Safety equipment (horn, lights, etc.) also had to be set up, each running on its own battery. Then, along the entire length of each of the tunnels, the newly constructed air ducts needed to be put into place.

Progress was slow. It was so cold that December that ice formed on the ladders, and each day the men had to spend time chipping it off. As well, the engine for the pump cut out frequently, requiring much time be spent rigging ways to bypass the problems.

A power vice is installed underground in Hedden's Shaft to begin drilling out from the tunnels at various angles.

Looking down Hedden's Shaft (Money Pit). Hoist track can be seen on the side. The water in the shaft is at sea level.

On December 14, Karl Graeser came to the island to tour the tunnels with Dad. They went down Hedden's Shaft, along the Hamilton tunnel, and down the Halifax tunnel for about 50 feet toward the cherry tree, which grew above them on the surface. Here they found fresh water seeping in. This would later prove to be a danger spot.

For days, my father, brother, and husband were totally occupied with preparing to work down in the Money Pit. They rigged gas tanks for the pump's engine, brought drums of gasoline up to the pit, and started the pump.

On December 21, they had to shut off the pump because it was too cold for the oil to run. Without oil as lubrication, the pump would burn up. Fortunately, the next day was warmer, and they were able restart it.

Karl Graeser and Bob Restall tour the underground work at the Money Pit.

Brook and Barry watch as 450 gallons per minute of sea water is pumped from the Money Pit.

Christmas Day saw everyone take a break from the work. The next day the pump was started up again, but things did not go smoothly at all. On December 27, Bobby wrote in his journal, "Got things ready to put air ducts to tunnel mouth. Chopped lots of ice off walls and platforms between 20 [and] 35 foot levels. Water going down very slowly. Put one duct in tunnel. Tried, without much luck to fix leak of 12th joint (in pump) in evening. Ice chunks falling down quite often."

Finally, their preparatory work was complete. In the margin of Bobby's journal on December 28, he wrote: "Start Treasure Hunting."

A window was cut in the side of the tunnel and the men prepared to drill out sideways in search of the old Truro Shaft #6, where it was thought the treasure had fallen through the spruce platforms. The journal entries for the days that followed list the holes drilled and what they found (blue clay, yellow clay, planks, etc.).

On January 1, they were still drilling, but the pump couldn't keep ahead of the water. They tried a temporary repair, but then the pump quit totally. They managed to fix it and were able to continue work, but for two days both the pump and the drill would cut out from time to time.

On January 3, they received a letter from Mr. Chappell stating that since there had been no treasure recovery, there would be no new contract.

Dad, Bobby, and Doug continued to work through January 4, but on the 5th the pump could not work fast enough to keep the water out of the pit. They went ashore for flashbulbs and to phone Tobias to advise him of Chappell's decision. By the time they returned, sufficient water had been pumped out of the pit, so they put their drill up in a new location and went for dinner. But when they returned, the water level was too high again. They splashed their way through the tunnels and took photographs every few feet — some 15 photos in all. Then they shut down the pump.

The next day Doug and I started loading up our Ambassador station wagon for the long ride home. We had been on the island for just over five months. We were sad to leave, but it looked to us as if the search for treasure on Oak Island could go on and on indefinitely. It was time for us to go home and pick up our old lives again, and for the treasure-hunting Restalls to face a new year on Oak Island — if they could convince Chappell to extend their contract yet again.

Chapter Fourteen

Time Stands Still

In January of 1963, my father had no contract to work on the island, his money was almost gone, and there were no new investors on the horizon. Again.

Looking back at 1962, the publicity they received had brought a small amount of new money and a stream of people who wanted to take over as the Oak Island treasure hunters.

Chappell had brought a Mrs. Frazer to the island. She used an unorthodox divining method, much like water-witching, to detect metals under the surface. She found indications that copper, gold, and silver lay everywhere underground. Dad's goodwill evaporated when she insisted that she needed to work at the Money Pit.

It is clear, from a description of Mrs. Frazer in Dad's letter to Fred Sparham, dated May 20, that Dad did not at believe in the woman's methods:

> Chappell brought a woman over who had a secret sort of metal finder. She has been back twice since. Mildred calls her Witch

Hazel, and it's more fun that a barrel of Monkeys. She runs around dangling a piece of plastic hose (clear) with a piece of metal in it that looks like a steel and brass plum bob. She has the whole lot hanging from a chain. She also has a gadget she takes out of a bag that looks like a pair of horns. Then she puts these horns against her forehead and goes around like a Moose. You just can't believe it at all."

With Dad's agreement, Chappell had let another treasure hunter, Johnson, dig on a different part of the island while Dad was at the Money Pit. Dad hoped this would take the edge off Chappell's desire to try something more. But it didn't.

That summer, a man from Oklahoma had really aroused Chappell's interest. This man flew to Nova Scotia in his own plane and visited the island with his pilot/bodyguard, his son, and Mr. Chappell. Through gritted teeth, Dad played gracious host.

Now, in January 1963, Chappell seemed inclined to let this man have a try. But the man's plan was to dragline the island and put all the dug material through a giant screen to separate earth and treasure. That kind of operation would destroy precious artifacts and ruin the island. There would be no more shafts or tunnels to testify to the long treasure-hunting history of Oak Island; no chance of ever seeing any more "original" work; no chance of ever seeing the treasure as the pirates had left it.

Water Witching

"Water witching" and other divining methods have long been used to locate underground resources. It is used with great success to find underground collections of water, thereby indicating a good place to drill a well. A "water witch," also known as a "dowser," uses a tree branch where it forks into two smaller branches creating a Y shape. Holding those smaller branches and pointing the thicker branch ahead, the witch walks across the land until the branch suddenly, of its own volition, points to the ground. Water will be found deep underground at that spot. There is no known scientific basis for it, but in skilled hands, the method works. Thin, metal, L-shaped rods are used in place of Ys by some modern water witches.

Both Dad and Chappell wanted to save the island, but Chappell was running out of patience. By that time the two were barely speaking, and David Tobias stepped in to try to smooth the troubled waters. In a meeting in mid-January, Dad pleaded his case — the pump's inability to remove sufficient amounts of water from the Money Pit had kept him from reaching the treasure. Chappell agreed to renew Dad's contract on the condition that he bring in something better to drive the pump. The new contract would end on June 30.

So a diesel generator that had once been in a Canadian Navy destroyer was purchased. It was much more powerful than the gasoline engine they had used up until then. It took not only the generator, but also a large electrical panel and other equipment to complete the new setup. Fred Sparham had located the generator, and his son Eddie told me that it was so heavy that when they loaded it onto the back of their truck, the front wheels came off the ground.

The generator was brought from Hamilton to the east coast by transport truck. Dad and Bobby transferred it to the barge by laying out rows of narrow steel pipes and then pushing the generator with a bulldozer until it rolled over the pipes and onto the boat. To move the generator from Smith's Cove up to the Money Pit, they purchased a huge old truck.

Every step of this new setup took days of exhausting effort. Once in place the generator worked, but not as well as they had hoped, and specialized mechanics had to be called to the island countless times to repair it. It was June 5 before the generator was ready to do its job. Dad's contract with Chappell was due to expire in just 25 days.

David Tobias urged my father to keep Mr. Chappell informed about progress and suggested that a tour might be a good idea. But the new equipment had drained the finances and Dad didn't even have enough money to buy the fuel to put on a show of the new generator's capacity. Tobias advanced him enough money to purchase 14 drums and Dad and Bobby worked day and night to prepare for the visit.

After weeks of rain, the clearing was slippery with mud, so, in the evening, three days before the visit, while wrestling drums of diesel fuel up off the truck flatbed, Dad slipped and fell. A drum full of fuel fell from the truck and landed on his leg. But he was lucky — his leg was painful, stiff, and bruised, but not broken.

Two days later, on June 19, Tobias and Chappell arrived on the island. Chappell had never been on the island when the pump was running and he was delighted. So delighted, in fact, that he agreed to extend Dad's contract until the end of the year. Tobias agreed to cover the fuel costs during that time. Everyone was happy.

> ## Sand in the Inlet Tunnel
> Through many years of treasure-hunting, the original inlet water tunnel had been so damaged that it no longer screened out all the sand as seawater passed through the reservoir. Some sand was getting through and gradually accumulating in the tunnel.

The next day, Dad and Bobby resumed drilling in the Money Pit and, almost immediately, instead of encountering hard clay, they hit beach sand. That caused great excitement, as it indicated that their drill had found the spot where the original inlet water tunnel joined the Money Pit.

But the next day, the pump shaft snapped and water immediately began to rise in the Money Pit. Bobby and Dad had to evacuate immediately. Later, in a letter to Frank Sparham, Dad described the event:

> Today we took the diamond (drill) and everything needed down. We got all set up and in the same hole and only a few inches of progress when the shaft snapped. Mildred heard the change of racket at once and nearly had a fit. We got everything out of the way and loaded in the (hoist) car in time. Could have done it faster but you know how these sudden emergencies are, both of us tried to do what the other fellow had been doing. We soon saw that was no good so we just went back to loading the (hoist)

car as if we were through for the day and let the hoist bring up the electric cable.

Something new was revealed through this shutdown, however. Back in January, when the pump was stopped, air bubbles had melted a hole in the ice that covered Chappell's Pond. That meant that not only were the 35-foot and 75-foot shafts connected to the Money Pit, but it seemed that Chappell's Pond was also part of that underground loop. Now, in June, as soon as the pump was shut down, air bubbles could be seen in the Cave-In Pit. It must be connected to the Money Pit, too.

By that time, more than 21 shafts had been put down by treasure hunters. An underground connection would be interesting if it involved only the "original" work — the Money Pit and the Cave-In Pit. But a connection between the "original" work and the treasure hunters' work (Chappell's Pond plus the two shafts) was not good news. It confirmed suspicions that the entire end of Oak Island was riddled with an underground network of interconnected passages. This would make the ground unstable and intensify the hazards of working underground.

Bob and Dad carried on, repairing the pump, but the diesel generator still ran hot and the Halifax mechanics had to keep coming back. Underground work lurched slowly ahead.

Do you remember the auger that went through what was thought to be a cement vault and brought up a piece of parchment? At that time, the treasure hunters (Truro Company) had been using a drill without a casing. When they tried to retrace the path to drill into the vault again, they couldn't do it. They realized that because they had used no casing, their drill must have been deflected by a rock or some other hard object, and had veered off in who-knows-what direction. The cement vault, which was imagined to be full of gold, jewels, and important documents, was not found again.

Dad and Bobby knew where Oak Island Treasure Company's drill had been placed when it made that discovery and they knew how long the drill rod had been. It was now their intention to drill out from the bottom of the Money Pit at all levels and angles that possibly could have been covered by that earlier, flexible drill. They were confident that this would bring them to the cement treasure vault. In the midst of this, Karl Graeser paid another visit to the island. He stayed for more than a week and worked alongside the men as they devised a cooling system. Graeser also put in some money, but more importantly he promised to cover the $400 a month needed for general expenses (to cover food, naphtha, propane, etc.) until the end of December. What a relief! Money for big purchases or machine-shop work still had to be found, but between Tobias and Graeser, costs for nonstop work in the Money Pit were now covered until December 31, 1963.

Dad and Bobby continued drilling at all levels and angles, and recorded all that they encountered. But one result was totally unexpected: while drilling down in the Money Pit, the drill entered a void (air space); then, a little farther down, it went through solid clay, then through another void and again more clay. Years earlier, William Chappell had found the same thing, but at different levels. Dad and Bobby at once realized that this must be a spiral tunnel. Chappell must have drilled down one side of the tunnel, and they had drilled down the other. The voids encountered created a pathway that spiralled down. At the bottom, and exactly due north, they found that the void widened into what they thought must be the walk-in tunnel. Before this discovery, Dad and Bobby did not believe that a walk-in tunnel existed. This evidence changed their minds. Dad made a sketch of how the spiral tunnel would look (see Figure 10, page 98).

Late in July, the men noticed that the cribbing in Hedden's Shaft had shifted drastically, and they were forced to stop drilling. A week's worth of precious diesel fuel was wasted keeping the pump running while they repaired and replaced the cribbing. They were able to resume drilling after the repairs were made, but on September 17, the pump shaft broke, this time very deep down (110 feet).

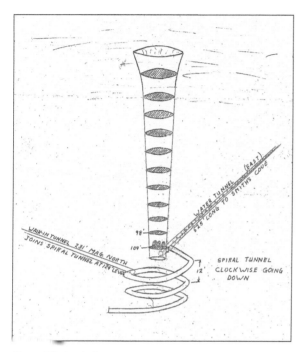

WATER TUNNEL (EAST) 626 LONG TO SMITHS COVE

WALK-IN TUNNEL 231' MAG. NORTH JOINS SPIRAL TUNNEL AT 124' LEVEL

98
104'

SPIRAL TUNNEL CLOCKWISE GOING DOWN
12'

Figure 10: A spiral tunnel leads off from the bottom of the Money Pit.

As Dad and Bobby removed the pump from the shaft, John Max, a soon-to-be-famous Canadian photographer, came to the island to take some pictures for a magazine article. He captured well the spartan existence, the grim determination, and the frustrations of the Restall search for treasure.

Though Dad and Bobby had a few spare parts stored on the island, many that they needed to repair the pump (for example, bearings) had to be custom-made at Hawbolts Machine Shop in Chester. Still others had to be bought in Hamilton by Fred Sparham and shipped to the island.

It was November 6 before the pump was finally ready, but it worked for less than 24 hours before seizing up and having to be taken apart again — apparently the new parts had fit too tightly.

Around that time, Dad wrote to Fred Sparham, telling him about his plans to continue the drilling and tunnelling. He had been unsuccessful in locating the cement vault, but he was sure that he could at last pinpoint the location of the Truro Company's Shaft #6 (the shaft where the wooded casks and boxes of treasure had spilled). In that letter, Dad enclosed photographs of hand-hewn timber (wood that was cut with an axe) made of spruce cut through by drill holes. He was sure that these pieces were from above and below the treasure of casks and boxes that had been discovered by the Truro Company in 1849 (at the time of the jewel on the auger). Dad and Bobby had come across these pieces of timber near Professor Hamilton's tunnel.

By the time Hurricane Ginny hit the east coast that year, the family had nailed lumber over the windows and taken other precautions, so they were spared

Dissembling the pump. Photo by John Max.

Evening in the Restall shack: Mildred, Rick, and Bobby.
Photo by John Max.

severe damage. The same could not be said for the wharf — every stick of wood
was carried away and all that remained was a pile of stones leading out into the
sea. Rebuilding would have to wait.

By the end of November, the pump was together again and they could hardly
wait to resume drilling. This time they would start from the floor of Professor
Hamilton's tunnel.

But the diesel generator was still overheating, and despite repeated visits by
the mechanics, they couldn't get it to run the pump smoothly and continuously.
It was clear that the electrical panel was contributing to this problem, but several
visits from the electrical engineers failed to correct anything. There were more
wires than there were places to attach them, but the engineers seemed unable to
explain or fix the problem.

By then the cold weather was fast approaching, and it was time to winterize
again. Cedar boughs were wrapped around the shacks and banked around the
top of the Money Pit to prevent freezing. Bobby made a note in his journal that

A piece of hand-hewn timber that had been part of the spruce platform under the casks and boxes of treasure in the Money Pit. A drill hole, probably made by the Truro Company, can be seen at the top end. It would have weakened the platform, which might have been the reason the treasure spilled into the tunnel and deep into the Money Pit in 1849.

Chappell seemed serious about letting the man from Oklahoma have a try at the treasure. It was a depressing time: the weather was against them, the machinery kept breaking down, and little progress was being made.

Bobby's journal entry from December 19, 1963, reveals the hardship of working through the winter: "Snow storm and wind 8 [inches] deep. Got six barrels on truck and part way up hill and engine broke down. Won't turn over. Valve covers off and looks okay. Could be broken valve jamming piston. Got two barrels up via car and toboggan. Drained diesel to get messes straightened before we try again. Pipes freeze fairly fast."

Still they pressed on.

Dad and Bobby had been able to drill out from the base of Hedden's Shaft, but drilling from tunnels, or digging new ones, could not be done safely by Dad and Bobby alone. One man was needed on top, and one man cannot work alone underground. For safety reasons, and for speed, they needed a work crew. Snowstorms and bitter cold interfered with their first attempts to bring men from the mainland, but on December 28 they were successful.

The group moved fuel drums up to the clearing, built frames for the tunnel, and started their work down in the pits. New Years Day came and went, and because they had plenty of fuel on the island, work in the shafts and tunnels continued.

Bobby beside the new air ducts in the Money Pit tunnels.

The work crew arrives at the surface after a hard day underground.

My mother wrote the following about those early days in 1964:

> Winter was on us and it was too cold to leave the diesel shut off for five hours and expect it to start up without a lot of trouble, so we had to enclose it.
>
> The men built a room around the diesel and put a small space-heater inside to be lit when the diesel was shut off....
>
> While the others were working down the pit, it was Bobby's job to do the running around. Check this, check that. Keep an eye on the diesel. Take the empty barrels to Chester by Boat.

Order supplies, bring back supplies. And if anything was needed down the pit, he loaded it on the hoist and sent it down. Signals were arranged so that he knew what was wanted….

Now that the ice was good and solid at the end of the island, the men could get to work without any trouble. But getting oil and supplies from Chester was another matter. Everything depended upon the weather. It was the deciding factor in getting the empty barrels to Chester to be filled with oil, and for the boatman being able to bring them back to the island.

It wasn't possible to carry full barrels in our small boat, so Bob arranged for a friend who had a 30-foot fishing boat to transport all oil and gas from Chester to the island. In order to carry as many barrels as possible, Gerald, our boatman, had put a deck on his boat and 12 to 14 barrels were loaded on top.

When they got to the island, a line was thrown to our shore and the barrels were tied on, then thrown overboard to be pulled in by our men. This was the only way we could get the fuel landed now that we no longer had a dock…. Several times the weather delayed delivery, and we needed a boat load at least every six days. We kept 500 gallons in reserve just in case and there were times when we dipped well into this reserve because of bad weather preventing delivery….

The men had been working down the pit for about 10 days when we had our first spot of real trouble. It was after lunch and everyone was getting into rubber suits ready to go below. Bob made the rounds as usual, checking the diesel and everything, including the motor room where the big generator was connected to the pump. As he opened the door, a cloud of smoke poured out and a grinding racket could be heard all over the clearing. A bearing had seized up. That meant the pump had to be stopped and taken apart. Unfortunately, all the tools were down the pit, and on top of that, the tunnel they were working on had to be boarded up. It was a new tunnel and was across the pit from the hoist. To board up the end of the tunnel would take quite some time, but it had to be done, otherwise the whole end would collapse as soon as the pit filled up and the water started to wash soil in.

None of the men fancied going down without the pump operating, with water pouring in at 450 gallons a minute. But they went. The trouble was lights. If the diesel wasn't running there wouldn't be any lights so it was up to Bobby to keep it going without letting it overheat.

The cooling system for the diesel depended upon the water from the pit being pumped around the cooler. No pump, no water. Without the cold inflow the diesel got warmer and warmer. Bobby had cut down the revs as much as he dared but still it was getting too warm. He started to shovel snow in the cooling barrel. Then he called for his brother to help. They were barely holding their own, for Bobby had to keep running into the engine room to check the gauges. They used all the snow nearby and were having to go farther afield. Next, I was outside, shovelling like mad, heaping the snow inside the fence where it was in easy reach of the boys.

Finally, the long-awaited signal came. Up came the hoist, up came the men … looking very pleased with themselves. It had taken forty minutes to block the end of the tunnel and load the tools. By that time the water was washing over the cat-walk they were standing on.

Further Reading

More of my mother's stories about the family's time on the island can be found in Oak Island Obsession: The Restall Story.

A week or so later, they were forced to deal with another emergency down in the pits. Fuel ran out while the men were working and the pump stopped with a shudder. The horn sounded, alerting Bobby and Mom. Down in the pits it was pitch black. The men were calling for lights. Carefully, rung by rung, Bobby climbed down the long, slippery, ice-covered ladder to bring a flashlight to the men in the tunnels below.

The crew managed to pack up and get out of the pit before the water caught up with them. But what about the backup lights — those new, battery-run, super-bright emergency spotlights? Well, one of the men had plans for the evening, so he had begun packing up early. First to be loaded on the hoist at the bottom of the heap — the emergency lights!

Underground work continued until the end of January. During that time they got a fair distance in their freshly dug tunnel and probed out from it, but found the work too dangerous to continue. A couple of months earlier, in the middle of the night, they had been awakened by a loud boom. The next morning they could see the earth around the cherry tree had collapsed, leaving a large crater. The tunnel underneath the cherry tree, where fresh water had been detected, had collapsed.

Now there were more signs of deterioration underground. They would need to put in a lot of time shoring up the tunnels if they wanted them to be safe. All underground work was stopped.

Then an important letter arrived from David Tobias. He wrote that, as Dad knew, he had gone far beyond what he had promised to invest, but now it was time to call a halt; he did not wish to invest farther.

The news was disappointing, but no one could question that David Tobias had done his share. He made no further investments of money, but he stayed actively involved behind the scenes.

In March, Dad wrote to Sparham to advise him that Mr. Chappell had decided to sell the island. If the Oklahoma man wanted to dragline the island, he'd have to buy it first. Chappell had set a price in dollars plus percentage of any treasure recovered, but he had changed the figures several times. It was hard to tell if he really meant to sell. Regardless, Dad headed for Hamilton, hoping to raise money to buy the island himself, but the response was not encouraging.

It was May before Dad had a new contract — it had been extended until the end of 1964. A few investments came in, but not the kind of money that would keep the hungry pump fed. Dad and Bobby returned to work at the beach.

Their careful drilling in the Money Pit in search of the vault was complete, but had failed to locate the treasure. It had yielded clear signs of where they should concentrate their next efforts, but repairs to the tunnels were essential before underground work could resume.

As long as they were on the island, Mom, Ricky, and Carney continued their explorations.

In July they finally learned that the electrical panel for the new pump setup had been faulty all along. That was what had caused the overheating and other problems with the diesel generator. The manufacturer of the panel had finally found the correct schematic for it (a schematic is like a map for electrical wires showing which connects to what). With the schematic and their top trouble-shooting electrical engineer, the problem was finally fixed, but the error had cost my dad almost a year of precious time and money.

Dad and Bobby renewed their efforts to find the inlet drain at the beach. They knew that the original five finger water inlet drain had been disturbed by

China pieces found buried in a trench close to the shoreline at Smith's Cove. Probably buried by pirates to hide evidence they had been there. Here, glued together,

Bob Restall drilling at the Cave-In Pit after it had been pumped dry.

too many treasure hunters, so blocking it off was no longer an option. They also believed that the pirates had put in a curving bypass drain at the edge of the beach to act as a second way to flood the Money Pit. This bypass drain originated near the Vertical Shaft and curved one way and then another toward the Cave-In Pit.

During their search they came across a trench they were convinced had been dug by the pirates. In it they found pieces of china. Dad believed that pirates must have buried the pieces to hide all signs that they had lived on the island.

My father sent the picture to Fred Sparham, commenting, "It's interesting.

But it's not treasure," and urged Fred to try to find one last big investor, for then they would be out of shares (of the treasure) to sell.

That fall, having no money to run the diesel generator, they focused their attention on the beach. They decided to clear it down to the clay level on a line that started at the white granite hand-drilled stone at the beach, passed through the Cave-In Pit, and went on to the Money Pit. Soon the beach was a sea of mud. They then cleared a swath of brush from the beach up to the Cave-In Pit.

In October, they set up the drill at the Cave-In Pit, pumped it out, and found what they believed was the bypass drain about 90 feet down. They spent several weeks there before they were forced to conclude that they would not be able to block the drain at this location. Many attempts by treasure hunters to cut off the sea water inlet drain had damaged this drain as well as the main inlet drain in Smith's Cove. Enough sand had come in to spoil any chance of using concrete as a plug, but not enough to block the flow of water. A more undisturbed place on the inlet tunnel would have to be found.

Dad and Bobby went back to the beach, where they worked until December, when Dad left for Hamilton in hopes of raising more money.

Chapter Fifteen

1965

Back in May of 1964, a reporter had come to the island and prepared a lengthy piece about Oak Island that appeared in *Reader's Digest* right after Christmas 1964.

The new year began with no contract, no money — and mounds of mail. Ablaze with excitement after reading the *Readers' Digest* article, hundreds of people wrote to my parents offering advice on how to raise the treasure. Some wanted a hefty portion of the treasure in exchange for their information; some asked for nothing but recognition.

My parents found the uproar bewildering. Letters came in from students in Denmark, from miners in Africa, from engineers in Australia, Germany, Canada, and the United States, from housewives around the world, and, seemingly, from anyone else who could lift a pen. Some communications seemed dashed off in haste, while it was obvious that others had been prepared with great care, some even containing detailed diagrams drawn to scale.

Many of the methods suggested were either impossible, had already been tried, or were ruled out as too costly (for instance, freezing the surrounding earth). Everyone had a theory about how the treasure could be raised. At first my parents answered each letter, but they just couldn't keep up with the avalanche of mail.

Many people who wrote were misinformed about the layout of Oak Island. To set the record straight, Bobby finished off his winter evening project — a map of the end of the island that contained the Money Pit, treasure hunters' shafts, and other landmarks (see Figure 1, page 15). He had the map reproduced and sold copies for one dollar.

Mr. Chappell received his share of this frenzied activity, as well. He soon tired of all the telegrams and letters — and the phone calls in the middle of the night — from people eager to replace the Restalls. His appetite for change had vanished. He told everyone the island was already under contract to Bob Restall. He provided Dad with details of all those who contacted him, and sent along copies of his responses.

All this attention, but no new investment money was coming in.

As mentioned earlier, when the treasure was reached, the government would get five percent of it and Mr. Chappell and my father would split the remainder 50/50. Through the years, Dad had sold investors parts of his share to keep the treasure hunt going. Some contracts were for as little as one quarter of one percent.

Now, to pay for future work, they needed a substantial investment. They contacted people who had invested in the search and asked them to give back a sliver of their percentage so there would be something to sell to raise new money. Fred Sparham told his son, Eddie, "Ten percent of something is still better than twenty-five percent of nothing." Even Mr. Chappell contributed by generously donating 30 percent of his share.

And just to set the record straight, the rumour that my father sold percentages until he had nothing left for himself is untrue. Through all those years of hardship and sacrifice, Dad vowed that no investor would end up with a bigger share than he did. He never budged on that.

Second-to-last beach shaft (spring, 1965). Each new shaft was larger than the last.

Anyway, by January 20 this was the new playing field: the Oklahoma man had run out of money and no longer had interest in Oak Island; Chappell was rumoured to be on the verge of bankruptcy; Dad now possessed a contract that ran until December 31, 1965.

All they needed was someone to come in with a bankroll.

Then suddenly, late in May, a new investor came in with $2,000. He also spent some time on the island and worked alongside Dad, Bobby, and Karl Graeser, who was visiting for a few days. The money was enough to pay off some debts and to keep the beach work going.

On June 29, Mr. Chappell wrote to my dad, telling him that a California geologist, Robert Dunfield, had contacted him asking for the contract for 1966. When Dunfield learned he could not get the island for himself, he approached Dad directly, with Chappell's approval.

And so, on July 3, Robert Dunfield wrote to my dad, introducing himself; on July 13 they met face-to-face; and on July 15 a contract was signed. Dunfield was in for $5,000. Soon after, Dan Blankenship offered to invest the same amount, but was turned away. My father had enough money. He knew precisely where the bypass tunnel could be blocked — it was at that spot where the oozy earth, "like porridge," had been encountered. Now was the time to put this hard-won knowledge to work. He was ready to block the tunnel and go after the treasure.

A new shaft was dug, and arrangements were made to bring a bulldozer to the island to strip down the earth to the clay level on a path leading to and beyond the new shaft.

On August 11, the bulldozer arrived on the island.

Through all his years on the island, Bobby had gone to the mainland on Saturday nights. Only the severest weather ever kept him away. By now he had made many good friends, and had become a regular participant in the popular, regional, Saturday-night stock car races. Aided by tips and advice exchanged through letters from his Hamilton high school shop teacher, Michael Farrell, Bobby put together a white Ford stock car that some dubbed "the tank." Now, at last, in August 1965, Bobby left the island on a Sunday, and with his trusty white Ford tank, he raced and earned two first-place finishes. Bobby's first. Ever.

On Sunday, August 15, his journal reads, "Dozer hitting more soft material. Down about 10 feet. I went racing. Two firsts."

That Bobby would write anything so personal in the Oak Island journal was rare. It was an important moment. He was pleased. Things were really going his way.

Two days later, on August 17, Smith's Cove was abuzz with activity. The bulldozer was scraping a deep pathway from the beach, past the beach shack, heading up toward the Cave-In Pit, and the pump was pulling water from the bottom of the freshly-dug shaft located partly up the hill. Bobby was working near the beach shack with Andrew Demont, Leonard Kaizer, and Cyril Hiltz — young, local men who were helping Bobby to clear brush and burn it in an empty 50-gallon drum that sat on the shoreline. Both Dunfield and Karl Graeser were also on site.

The air was electric with optimism and urgency.

My father needed to take the boat over to mainland so he could visit his bank in Chester before closing time — papers had to be signed before Dunfield's funds could be released. Dad was running late, but before he went up to the cabin to change his clothes for the trip ashore, he decided to take one last look in the new shaft to see how well the pump was getting rid of water.

This newest shaft was behind the beach shack at a point where the land had started to rise to go up to the clearing. The shaft was large and deep (10 feet by 30 feet by 27 feet deep) and had three or four feet of water in the bottom.

Dad peered down into the shaft, and without a sound, he tumbled in.

Bobby saw it happen, dropped the bushes he had in his hands, and raced over to help. Others did, too. Bobby started down the ladder, but suddenly fell into the shaft. Karl Graeser was right behind Bobby, and began to climb down, but he lost consciousness and slid into the shaft, too. Cyril Hiltz followed Karl, and Cyril's cousin, Andrew Demont, was close behind. Leonard Kaizer was the last man to rush in to help the others.

One-by-one, as each man tried to climb down the ladder into the shaft, he lost consciousness and fell in.

Ed White, a fireman from Buffalo, was visiting the island that day with a group of friends. He heard the cries for help and rushed to the shaft. His wife pleaded with him not to go down, but White tied a handkerchief around his face and had someone lower him into the shaft. He was able to get a rope around Leonard Kaizer, so that those at the top could pull him out. Then White went after Andrew Demont, who was unconscious with his arms locked around a steel pipe, which supported him above water.

Even in his unconscious state, Demont lashed out and punched White. But the fireman prevailed and got the rope harness around him so that he could be pulled from the shaft.

Ed White was a hero. He saved Leonard Kaizer and Andy Demont that day. But he could do no more. By then, he, too, was feeling the effects of the invisible gas.

On that fateful day, August 17, 1965, Cyril Hiltz, Karl Graeser, Bob Restall, Sr., and Bob Restall, Jr. all lost their lives. The coroner's ruling was "death by drowning."

Later, while Andrew Demont was in hospital in Halifax, Ed White visited him and told him that the water had been up to Demont's lips by the time White was able to secure him in the rope-harness.

Demont told me that at the top of the shaft he could smell nothing, but that as he started down the ladder, a foul-smelling odour had overwhelmed him. As he looked into the shaft he could see Karl Graeser sitting underwater, with only the very top of his head showing. Andrew said he saw Bobby, his eyes closed, supporting his dad's head just above the waterline. Andrew said he placed his hand on Bobby's shoulder, and then he, too, drifted into unconsciousness. Apparently he stayed like that as the water slowly rose around him, until Ed White came to rescue him.

Many years later I was told that the gas that overwhelmed the men was probably hydrogen sulphide, a lethal gas that can form when rotting vegetation is combined with salt water. Apparently, it can be odourless or have a foul rotten-egg smell, depending on the concentration.

There is no doubt in my mind that there was salt water in the ground near the new shaft. Right beside it were two tall apple trees. The apples that grew on those trees looked like a type we call "Transparents" in Ontario. Those two trees looked exactly like others on the island, but they bore delicious, crisp, tangy fruit, whereas apples from similar trees were tasteless. A local woman told me that when apple trees grow near the sea in a mix of fresh water and salt water, they produce juicy, sharp, flavourful apples.

Could the salt water that nurtured those apples have reacted with the coconut fibre, eel grass, and other old vegetation that had lain dormant for so long in the pirates' beachwork, producing the deadly hydrogen sulphide? Could the "porridge-like" earth that was encountered only at this location on the island be in some way related to this toxic combination?

We may never know.

I find it ironic that my father should die this way. He was so safety-conscious that everything he built was two or three times stronger than necessary. We joked that his carnival rides were likely to sink through to China if a heavy rain ever hit. And everything he built was grounded, vented, and had backup systems.

On the other hand, my father was so obsessed with Oak Island that I had remarked to my husband as we left the island three years earlier that the only way my father would ever leave Oak Island was "feet first." I had meant that he

Carney, waiting at the death pit. Photo by C. Prazak.

would find one way or another to hang on and keep trying until he died from old age. I certainly did not mean this.

Karl Graeser was a fine man with a wife and two daughters who deeply loved him. He was a successful businessman who was enthusiastic, adventuresome, and always ready to lend a hand. A terrible loss.

And Cyril Hiltz. He was no treasure hunter. He didn't sign on to risk his life. He came to the island that day only to earn a few dollars. But when that crucial moment came, he rushed in to help the others. He was only 16 years old. His loss is especially cruel.

My father, Robert Ernest Restall, had lived a rich and varied life — the life he wanted. He was 60 years old. Not nearly enough time, but they were 60 good years.

My brother Bobby, Robert Keith Restall, is another matter. Twenty-four is too young to die. Bobby was smart and funny and always upbeat. He never had a chance. My brother deserved better than this.

But, of course, they all did.

Chapter Sixteen

The Aftermath

A lot of time has passed since that fateful day in August of 1965.

I visited Oak Island a few months ago. Surprisingly, it felt really good to be there. Parts of the island, untouched by the lust for gold, are still beautiful. As I walked, I thought to myself, *This is a good place. More than good. It is a wonderful place.*

But at the far end of the island — the Money Pit end — everything is different. The beaches have been scraped bare. The clearing, no longer a high, flat expanse, has been gouged out and re-formed into lopsided, jagged terrain. The Money Pit, once part of a 32-foot-high plateau, now sits on misshapen, uneven land, almost down to sea level. That end of the island is ugly, ruined.

At home I pull out old photographs and letters and journals. I want to remember a time before the accident, before the deaths, a time when all of Oak Island was a beautiful and happy place; the time when my father, mother, and brothers first came to the island.

They had been brimming with enthusiasm. They were embarking on a wonderful adventure, and the Restalls just might be the ones to solve this baffling, centuries-old puzzle. Here was a shot at fortune and fame. They lived in a bubble of good wishes, good cheer, and boundless expectations. It was an extraordinary time, when anything seemed possible.

Of course, there was also the back-breaking labour and the endless frustration, but after all, what's an adventure without adversity?

I try to hang on to the good memories of Oak Island, but darker images keep creeping in — the disappointments and obstacles, one-by-one, year after year, that gradually wore the family down. In time, the hunt for treasure crowded out all else in their lives. Nothing mattered but Oak Island and its treasure — at least for my dad.

Oak Island does that. Men go there seeking riches and fame, and forget who they are. During my family's final year, only my father was still steadfast in his belief in the Restall hunt for treasure. By that time, conversations among the four of them were strained. Doubts, disagreements, and long silences had settled in.

The hunt for treasure was like a job that took every thought, every bit of energy, every cent. Day after day, nothing but drab, drone-like hard work — no glamour here. It seemed to my mother and brothers that this job was one that would never be finished.

Until it *was* finished — but with such a horrible ending.

After the Accident

Before we run out of pages, I want to tell you a little of what happened to my family after the accident.

My mother moved to a small house in Western Shore. Her first concern was finding a way to support herself and Ricky. Being an ex-dancer, motorcycle rider, and treasure-hunter was not likely to open any doors, so she decided to go back to school. She enrolled in a business course in Bridgewater and began her first studies since she was 12 years old.

Soon she earned a diploma in typing, shorthand, and accounting, and was hired to work in a medical clinic.

Ricky had been on the island from age nine to 14, mostly in the company of adults — family members and visiting tourists — but hardly ever with anyone his own age. Life on the mainland, with the give and take and bumps and bruises of high-school life was a challenge. But he survived. In time he became a carpenter, and is alive and well and living in Ottawa.

My mother made a new life for herself. She remained fiercely independent, but between a job she loved and her neighbours, she formed friendships that were deep and lasting.

Of course, she missed Dad and Bobby terribly. My mother and dad had been a perfect match, and my mother and brother had always shared a special bond. Bobby's death was especially hard on her. My mother felt responsible. One day, before the accident, Bobby had taken all he could of Oak Island. After a heated argument with Dad, Bobby packed up and left. My mother had gone after him and convinced him to return — his dad needed him. She rarely spoke of it, but that weighed heavily on her for the rest of her years.

My mother never left the east coast. She was 90 years old when she died. For the last 38 years of her life, she lived in a small house on a hill, in the community of Western Shore, where, from her living room window, she could look out and see Oak Island.

Treasure Hunters Who Followed the Restalls

When I started this book, I intended to tell the full Oak Island story, including those treasure hunters who came after the Restalls. But space will not allow it, so we will have to be satisfied with the briefest of highlights.

- **Robert Dunfield** was the first treasure hunter after the accident. He had a causeway built connecting the mainland to Oak Island. It allowed mammoth equipment to be moved over to the island.

  Down at the Money Pit end of the island, no work was done to stop the sea water, but the huge machinery moved soil from this place to that in search of the treasure. The work gouged out part of the clearing so that the Money Pit, which had been 32 feet above sea level, was reduced to just 10 feet. His work drastically changed the terrain, giving free rein to the incoming sea water. It turned that end of the island into a huge heap of slippery mud. No treasure was found.

- Dan Blankenship and David Tobias formed **Triton Alliance Limited**, the next treasure-hunting company. After drilling countless exploratory holes, they put down a mammoth caisson; Dan climbed down inside, but the caisson began to slowly collapse, threatening to crush the life out of him. He barely escaped. Before this near-fatal event, Triton had located and videotaped what many believe to be evidence of treasure within a huge cavern beneath the bedrock of the island. Their video also revealed what appears to be a human hand.

- **Oak Island Tours Inc.**, the final treasure-hunting company, is still at work on Oak Island. In fact, they have only just begun. This company includes a previous Oak Island treasure hunter, Dan Blankenship, and four newcomers from Michigan — Craig Tester, Marty Lagina, Rick Lagina, and Alan J. Kostrzewa. It is reported that they possess adequate financing to see the job through to a successful end.

  I've exchanged emails with one of these men from Michigan and met face-to-face with another, and I'm convinced that they respect the island and the searchers who went before them and that they will give their search for treasure their very best effort. I wish them every success.

But if these men are not successful, well then, I have to ask —Would YOU step in? Could YOU be the one to solve the mystery and find the treasure of Oak Island?

Appendix 1

Timeline

1795	Daniel McInnis, John Smith, Anthony Vaughan
1804–05	The Onslow Company
1849–50	The Truro Company
1861 65	The Oak Island Association
1866–67	The Eldorado Company of 1866 (a.k.a. The Halifax Company)
1878	Mrs. Sophia Sellers accidentally discovers the Cave-In Pit
1893–99	The Oak Island Treasure Co. (Frederick Blair)
1909–11	The Old Gold Salvage Company (Captain Henry Bowdoin)
1931	William Chappell
1934	Thomas Nixon
1935–38	Gilbert Hedden

1938–44	Professor Edwin Hamilton
1951	Mel Chappell and Associates
1955	George Green
1958	William and Victor Harman
1959–65	Robert Restall
1965–66	Robert Dunfield
1969–2006	Triton Alliance (David Tobias and Dan Blankenship)
2006	Oak Island Tours Inc. (Marty Lagina, Rick Lagina, Craig Tester, Alan J. Kostrzewa, and Dan Blankenship)

Appendix 2

SKETCH OF RESERVOIR 1961
APART FROM GREAT AMOUNT
OF LABOUR. THE
PLANNING & SUPERVISION
ARE OUTSTANDING
IT IS INCREDIBLE

STONE FOUNDATION APROX 10' WIDE

CLEARED FOR BOATS

PRESENT WHARF BUILT 1937 IN LOCATION OF 3 EARLIER ONES

RESERVOIR 5' of LARGE ROCKS
140'
MOSTLY TORN APART 1850
90% of BOULDERS STILL HERE

END 1850 COFFER DAM

LOW TIDE

241' WIDE

RESERVOIR 5' of LARGE ROCKS
MOSTLY NOT TORN UP

1704 DATED STONE IN PAVING OVER SEAL

SEAL

HIGH TIDE

PAVED WITH ASSORTED BOULDERS & COVERED WITH EEL GRASS
(A) & COCOANUT to THIS LINE

HIGH TIDE

PAVED AREA TO PROTECT SEALS & RESERVOIR

RESERVOIR 5' of LARGE ROCKS
MOSTLY NOT TORN UP

FROM HERE BACK COVERED EEL GRASS & BRANCHES LOCAL WOOD

PAVED AREA TO PROTECT SEALS & RESERVOIR

NOTE
A - WHERE DRAINS CONVERGE
B. ROUND DRAIN TRACED TO HERE
C. FARTHEST INLAND PIRATES PAVING DISTURBED BY OTHERS.
FOUND ACORNS HERE WORK HERE DONE IN FALL OF YEAR BY PIRATES

VERTICAL SECTION

TO PREVENT EROSION SINGLE LAYER STONE PAVING

SEAL 5' TO 7' WIDE

PAVED AREA.

175'

SEAL STONE TIGHT PACKED WITH HARD CLAY

SEAL

5' DEEP RESERVOIR

SINGLE LAYER PAVING OVER WHOLE THING

Selected Reading

Crooker, William S. *The Oak Island Quest*. Hantsport, NS: Lancelot Press, Revised Edition, 1992.

Finnan, Mark. *Oak Island Secrets*. Halifax, NS: Formac Publishing, Revised Edition, 1997.

Harris, Graham, and Les MacPhie. *Oak Island and Its Lost Treasure*. Halifax: Formac Publishing, 2005.

Harris, Reginald V. *The Oak Island Mystery*. Toronto: Ryerson Press, June 1958.

Lamb, Lee. *Oak Island Obsession: The Restall Story*. Toronto: Dundurn Group, 2006.

O'Connor, D'Arcy. *The Secret Treasure of Oak Island*. Guilford, CT: The Lyon Press, 2004.

Sullivan, Randall. "The Curse of Oak Island." *Rolling Stone*. New York: January 2004.

Websites

If you become hooked on Oak Island, you will be amazed at the amount of material that is available to you on the Internet. Just search "Oak Island treasure," "Oak Island chronology," or "Oak Island pirates," and you will find riches beyond belief. There are historical pieces, opinion pieces "for" and "against," and even an interactive site that teaches and tests Oak Island history.

Happy hunting!

Chester Municipal Heritage Society. *www.chesterbound.com/heritage. htm.* If you have a chance to visit Nova Scotia, try to get to the village of Chester, an absolutely beautiful community by the sea. The Chester Municipal Heritage Society has mounted an excellent Oak Island exhibit in the old Chester Train Station. Danny Hennigar, Curator, Carol Nauss, Chair, and society members and volunteers are to be commended. The Restall 1704 stone is presently on display there.

The Friends of Oak Island. *www.friendsofoakisland.com.* This is a group of individuals who are working hard on behalf of Oak Island. They lead tours of the island during some weekends in the summer months and have created a superb exhibit of archival material on the island. And, because of their close relationship with the owners of Oak Island, their website contains the latest news of treasure-hunting activities taking place there. Garnette Blankenship and Charles Barkhouse have done much to keep the memory of the Restalls alive. They, and other Friends' members and volunteers are doing a great job on behalf of Oak Island and all of its treasure hunters.

Oak Island Treasure. *www.oakislandtreasure.co.uk.* This is a fantastic website about Oak Island that was started in England years ago by Jo Atherton. She has made available several rare photographs and other fascinating archival material. Her collection is like no other, and you can always count on her forum for lively debate.

Index

Of Related Interest

BETRAYED: *The Legend of Oak Island*
by Christopher Dinsdale
978-1-894917919 / $10.95

Connor MacDonald and his mother have encountered Henry Sinclair, Norwegian prince and Earl of Orkney, who rescues them from highwaymen. Prince Henry is an adventurer who has sailed to the farthest reaches of the known world. Events soon lead Connor, now a squire, his friend Angus, and Prince Henry to the shores of Vinland and to Oak Island.

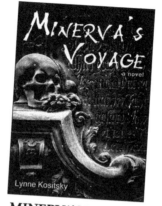

MINERVA'S VOYAGE

by Lynne Kositsky

978-1-554884391 / $12.99

Dragged off the streets of 17th-century England and onboard a ship bound for Virginia by the murderous William Thatcher, Noah Vaile befriends a young cabin boy, Peter Fence. After being shipwrecked on the mysterious Isle of Devils, the two set off on an adventure filled with mystery, danger, villainy, and a treasure rarer and finer than gold.

Available at your favourite bookseller.

DUNDURN
www.dundurn.com

What did you think of this book?
Visit www.dundurn.com for reviews, videos, updates, and more!